הגדה של פסח

Gates of Freedom:
A Passover Haggadah

by

Chaim Stern

Illustrations by

Andrea Meyer

Introduction by

Eugene B. Borowitz

Chaim Stern is Senior Rabbi of Temple Beth El of Northern Westchester. He has been the principal creator of the liturgy of Reform Judaism for the past quarter century, beginning with the publication of "Gates of Prayer." He is, in addition, creator of other works and Co-Editor of the liturgy of the British Liberal movement.

Eugene B. Borowitz is Professor of Education and Jewish Religious Thought at Hebrew Union College-Jewish Institute of Religion, author of many works on Jewish thought and life, and a leading theologian of contemporary Judaism.

Andrea H. Meyer earned a B.F.A. from Carnegie-Mellon University and is completing the M.F.A. program in Computer Graphics and Interactive Media at Pratt Institute. She is a Founding Principal of Emdash, Inc., in New York City.

Revised edition, Copyright © 1999 by Chaim Stern
Published by Behrman House, Inc.
www.behrmanhouse.com
Design: Emdash, Inc.

Managing Editor: Seymour Rossel

Library of Congress Cataloging in Publication Data

Haggadah (Reform, Stern)
(Hagadah shel Pesah) = Gates of freedom
English and Hebrew
Bibliography: p.
1. Reform Judaism-Liturgy- Texts. 2. Haggadah (Reform, Stern)-Texts.
3. Seder. I. Stern, Chaim. II. Meyer, Andrea H. III. Title. IV. Title: Gates of freedom.
BM675.P4Z667   296.4'37 81-84191
ISBN13: 978-0-87441-662-6   AACR2
Printed in the U. S. A.

Contents

Introduction

The Seder confounds our usual notions of "religion." It takes place at home, not in a sanctuary; is conducted by anyone or everyone, not by a rabbi; involves more eating than petitioning of God; requires us to drink more than we usually do yet isn't orgiastic; touches us with tales of a slavery we have not experienced and amazes us with Temple Rites we can hardly imagine; evokes so many family memories we can hardly think about Egypt; and gives us an opportunity for familial custom or community style that transforms a two-thousand-year-old rite into a living experience.

Some people think that great cosmic themes demand serious attention and meticulous observance. A Seder, I suppose, should have some element of high dignity running through it. But seated around the table, with family gathered from afar or, if not there, badly missed, with our annual guests and this year's invitees, I cannot help but put before me the Torah's general rule about the pilgrimage day observance: "…you shall rejoice in your festival." That is a command. We shall not have fulfilled our Jewish duty if we do not have a joyous time at the Seder.

How shall we do that? How shall we learn to be joyous while joining our people in their perennial service of God? In part, this Haggadah will help. It speaks of all the old ways in an idiom that preserves their ancient power yet addresses us who know ourselves to be as free a generation of Jews as ever lived. Again and again it suggests ways we might extend the Torah's message for this celebration deeper into our lives or further out into the world. With its many subtle interplays of tradition and modernity it lifts the spirits of all who know they must be Jews in old, familiar ways, yet somehow re-create the past in their personal fashion.

But we Jews do not believe that rites perform themselves, nor that their sacred power is unleashed merely in the doing. And surely this is true of the command to rejoice. Our contribution to this elegant text must be the creation of delight. One cannot give rules for being happy, which may be why the Rabbis limited their instructions about rejoicing. Having given us this incomparable context in which to fulfill our duty, they left the personal side largely to us. For me, elation has to do with smiling, with exchanging glances, with an occasional spontaneous comment about the text or the company, with loving what we are doing this evening and communicating that to everyone.

The real test of the evening's festivity, I suggest, lies less in being able to add to its pleasures than in overcoming its difficulties. What bothers you the most—long Hebrew passages? dry political interpolations about true freedom? relatives who repeat the same tiresome stories? matzah balls that come out too soft or too hard? people who can't stay on tune or don't like your favorite? They too are part of Jewish celebrating. Consider them, if you can, a challenge to your Jewish spirit and see if on this holiday you can find a way to sanctify what annoys you.

My model in all this is the great unwritten but perennially observed folk rite of the Seder: knocking over a glass of wine (perhaps breaking a beautiful crystal goblet in the process). Rarely does a tablecloth go unscathed through a Seder at our house—and we are lucky if our Haggadot and clothing escape the miniature deluge. I have long since given up the possibility that we could make this the Seder's equivalent of breaking a glass at a wedding; could we, then, work out ways of making it unlikely that wine would ever be spilled? Probably we could, but why bother? A little spilling and a stain or two are hardly enough to dampen our joy at not being slaves. And by now, we have gotten so used to them, that we consider them a part of the festivities. This too helps constitute that wonderful web which Judaism teaches us to weave, in order to integrate the ordinary and the metaphysical. Not every spill can become a part of our rejoicing; but knowing which ones are worth our seriousness is part of what each Seder and Judaism as a whole wish to teach us.

May you celebrate in high, human, holy joy.

Eugene B. Borowitz

CELEBRATING TOGETHER FROM AFAR? VISIT BEHRMANHOUSE.COM/SEDER FOR TIPS

Preface

Pesach

In the beginnings (1500-1200 B.C.E.) there were two Festivals: Pesach, a shepherds' holiday celebrating the lambing season, and Chag Hamatzot, a farmers' holiday celebrating the year's first grain harvest. And still the names are preserved: Passover, the Festival of Unleavened Bread.

In the second half of the thirteenth century Israel left Egypt, and thereafter the two celebrations became a single Festival with new meanings. Pesach came to be understood as referring to the last of the Ten Plagues, when God "passed over" (pasach = Pass over) the houses of the Israelites, and the unleavened bread came to recall the haste of Israel's departure, when there was no time for bread to rise. This single Festival became Z'man Cherutenu, "The Season of Our Freedom," commemorating Israel's deliverance from Egyptian bondage— a deliverance seen as the supreme paradigm of the divine redemptive power in human history. In Heine's words: "Since the Exodus, Freedom has always spoken with a Hebrew accent."

Passover, then, has four aspects. It is seasonal, a rejoicing in the annual reawakening of nature at springtime. It is historical, marking the "birthday" of the Jewish people. It is a festival of freedom. It is a ritual of preparation for an ultimate redemption, of which our first redemption was a hint and a promise.

The Seder

From very early times Pesach has been an occasion for public worship. It also gave rise to a more intimate celebration by families or groups of families. This took place, in ancient times, at a festival meal in which the paschal lamb was eaten together with bitter herbs and unleavened bread. After the destruction of the Temple in 70 C.E., the sacrificial system came to an end, and so the lamb—a sacrifice—was omitted, but the meal continued and attained even greater importance. It also became more elaborate. To the unleavened bread and bitter herbs, other dishes were added and invested with symbolic significance.

Closely associated with the meal is the duty of parents to teach their children about the Exodus, so that each generation of Jews relives that great experience and understands its meaning. So the Bible commands:

"Tell your child on that day" (Exodus 13:8). In time that command led to the creation of a well-defined ritual known as Seder Haggadah, "The Order of Narration." Later Ashkenazi (European) Jews came to use the term Seder for the ritual as a whole, including the meal, and the term Haggadah for the book itself, the telling of the Exodus story along with appropriate prayers and songs.

The Haggadah

The Haggadah as a book dates from the ninth century, when it was included in Jewish prayerbooks and law-codes. By the twelfth century it began to be published on its own. During the long centuries before its compilation as a book, the Haggadah was transmitted by word of mouth, a fluid text whose core was fixed but whose details varied from time to time, and from community to community.

The publication of the Haggadah as a volume in its own right resulted in the production of countless manuscript editions, of which a few have survived. Some of them are richly illuminated and illustrated. They are among the masterpieces of Jewish religious art.

Since the invention of printing in the fifteenth century, something like 3,000 printed editions have appeared. Essentially the same, they nevertheless show many variations according to local custom, while the emergence of Reform Judaism in the nineteenth century heralded a period of further diversification. Even Israeli Kibbutzim (some of them anti-religious) have produced their own versions of the ancient ritual. Of making many Haggadot there is no end!

This Haggadah

The aim of this Haggadah is to let the traditional text speak for itself, both in its original tongue and through a new translation, with only minor omissions, abridgments, and rearrangements. In addition, we aim to sharpen its significance for the modern Jew by the inclusion of supplementary passages, some drawn from Biblical and Rabbinic Literature, some from general literature, and some newly written. This Haggadah is offered in the hope that it will help those who use it to find renewed delight in the Seder, as they experience both familiar and unfamiliar levels of meaning, relevance, and inspiration.

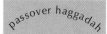

Preparation

Hospitality

Early in the Seder we say: "Let all who are hungry come and eat; let all who are in need come share our Passover." As an expression of this hospitality, it has long been customary to invite one or more guests. It is especially commendable to invite persons whose circumstances might otherwise prevent them from participating in a family Seder.

The Ritual

The person leading the Seder should study the Haggadah in advance and plan how it is to be used (leaving some room for spontaneity). Thus, some passages may be recited in English. Some may be spoken and others sung. Moreover, the Seder may be shortened by omitting some of the passages, or lengthened by supplementary readings from appropriate anthologies or by additional explanations and discussion. For the latter purpose, the Notes at the end of this volume should prove useful. They also give the sources of all passages.

The Meal

There is no standard or stipulated menu for the Seder meal, which is a matter of regional and family tradition, but the following are needed for the symbolic role they play in the Seder (their significance will be explained in the text):

1. WINE, red or white, in sufficient quantity to enable each participant's glass to be filled four times.

2. KARPAS, Green Herbs such as parsley, lettuce, chicory, celery, or any other green salad vegetable; a small quantity for each participant.

3. SALT WATER, in which the Green Herbs (KARPAS) will be dipped by each participant.

4. MATZAH, Unleavened Bread made from any one of the five species of grain, usually wheat, by a process which ensures that the flour is kept perfectly dry throughout.

5. ZEROA, a roasted shank-bone with some meat on it, reminiscent of the paschal lamb. (Therefore, some use a lamb bone; others use a beef or even a chicken bone.) As it is only for display, one is sufficient.

6. BEITSAH, an egg boiled, or first boiled and then roasted, in its shell. This too is only for display.

7. MAROR, Bitter Herbs, a small quantity for each participant. Though some use the leaves, stem, or main root of lettuce (CHAZERET), the most common practice is to use sliced or grated root of horseradish.

8. CHAROSET, a sweet paste in which the Maror is dipped, so that each participant will require a small quantity. Recipes vary but usually include (a) chopped or grated nuts; (b) chopped or grated apples or other fruit (especially those mentioned in the Song of Songs); (c) a little wine; (d) cinnamon or ginger. The latter (if used) should preferably be sliced into thin sticks, rather than grated, to symbolize the straw, as the rest symbolizes the clay, with which the Israelites were forced to make bricks in Egypt.

The Table

The Seder table should be given a festive appearance, with a white tablecloth and the best dishes and silver. The seasonal aspect of Pesach makes it appropriate to decorate the table with spring flowers. A candlestick holding two candles (more are permissible) should be placed in front of the person who is to kindle the lights.

In some communities there is a tradition—for which there is no very cogent reason but which may be felt to lend an extra touch of solemnity to the occasion—that the person who conducts the Seder wears a white robe called a Kittel. At certain points in the Seder, there is an old custom of "leaning" to the left; to facilitate this, the leader at least should be provided with a cushion: which serves also to remind us of the leisure, the ease, our forebears did not enjoy in many lands of bondage.

Every participant should be provided with a Haggadah, a wine-glass, a plate containing Karpas, Matzah, Maror and Charoset, and a bowl of salt water. In recent times, it has become customary to lay an extra place, or to keep an extra chair, as a reminder of those Jews who, living under an oppressive regime, are unable to celebrate the Seder in the traditional manner.

In front of the leader there should be: (1) a Seder plate or dish (k'arah) for the display of Karpas, Charoset, Maror, Beitsah and Zeroa; (2) a Matzah cover in the form of a napkin with three compartments, each containing one Matzah (Seder plates and Matzah covers are obtainable at synagogue Judaica shops or Jewish bookshops); (3) a extra glass or (preferably) silver goblet known as "The Cup of Elijah."

There are two customs concerning the Afikoman that should be kept in mind: (a) in many households the Afikoman is hidden by the leader; later on, the children are encouraged to look for it; (b) in other households, the children are encouraged to hide the Afikoman, and the leader must later find it. Both customs depend on the fact that the Seder meal concludes with the eating of the Afikoman, and that it cannot be completed without it. The leader should therefore bear in mind the need to have ready a prize or prizes for the child or children, with which to redeem the Afikoman.

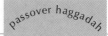

Acknowledgments

To the First Edition

As Editor of this Haggadah, I owe much to many. I especially thank Rabbi John D. Rayner, whose work has greatly influenced my own. Rabbi Rayner and I have collaborated in many liturgical works, from "Service of the Heart" (London, ULPS, 1967), to "A Modern Passover Haggadah" (London, ULPS, 1981), to "Siddur Lev Chadash" (London, ULPS, 1995). I owe much that is good in the present Haggadah to him, and here record my gratitude.

The following read the manuscript carefully and made many helpful suggestions: Rabbi Joan B. Friedman, Rabbi Lawrence A. Hoffman, Rabbi Sandra Levine, Rabbi Michael A. Robinson, Rabbi Julius Rosenthal, of blessed memory, and Susan Stern. Cantor Kenneth Cohen's assistance in matters related to music was invaluable. Ronald Feldman helped tremendously in various ways, and especially with regard to the art. Stanley Gluck expertly advised and assisted in all aspects of this book's design. Rabbi Miles Cohen of Bet Sha'ar Press, Inc. was always helpful and patient in the typesetting and associated matters. And Seymour Rossel was always forthcoming with useful advice and information: all have my grateful thanks.

Finally, I thank the many individuals of Temple Beth El of Northern Westchester who have used this Haggadah in mimeographed form (and especially Myra and Milton Schubin, in whose home we have celebrated the Passover with this Haggadah), and whose enthusiastic response has encouraged me to offer this Haggadah to the community at large.

To the Second Edition

In the fifteen years that have passed since the publication of this Haggadah, many more Haggadot have been published, but those thousands who have celebrated Pesach with the help of Gates of Freedom have encouraged me to believe that it has a place at their Seder table. Seymour Rossel's advocacy of this edition was crucial to its publication, and he has my grateful thanks, once again. I thank, in addition, MelvinWolfson, for his meticulous copy-editing, his encouragement, and his friendship.

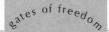
בדיקת חמץ | Searching for Leaven

There is a custom to search for any bread or other food containing leaven by the light of a lamp or candle after dark on the eve of the day before Passover—or, if that is a Friday, the preceding evening. Some is always found, because it is secreted beforehand to provide occasion for the (two-stage) ritual. We thus fulfill the words: "You shall eat unleavened bread for seven days; moreover, on the preceding day you shall remove all leaven from your houses" (Exodus 12.15).

On the following morning, the leavened food is burned or, preferably, fed to animals or birds.

The search for leaven is called "Bedikat Chametz," while the removal of leaven is called "Biur Chametz."

Before the search, the following is said:

זְכוֹר אֶת־הַיּוֹם הַזֶּה אֲשֶׁר
יְצָאתֶם מִמִּצְרַיִם מִבֵּית
עֲבָדִים כִּי בְּחֹזֶק יָד הוֹצִיא
יהוה אֶתְכֶם מִזֶּה וְלֹא יֵאָכֵל
חָמֵץ:

Zachor et hayom hazeh asher y'tzatem mimitzrayim, mibeit avadim; ki b'chozek yad hotzi Adonai et-chem mizeh; v'lo yei-a-cheil chameitz.

Remember this day, the day you went forth from Egypt, from the house of bondage; for with a mighty hand the Eternal God led you forth to freedom; no leavened bread shall be eaten.
(Exodus 13:3)

בָּרוּךְ אַתָּה יי אֱלֹהֵינוּ מֶלֶךְ
הָעוֹלָם, אֲשֶׁר קִדְּשָׁנוּ
בְּמִצְוֹתָיו וְצִוָּנוּ עַל בְּעוּר
חָמֵץ.

Ba-ruch a-ta Adonai, Eh-lo-hei-nu me-lech ha-o-lam, a-sher kid'sha-nu b'mitz-vo-tav v'tzi-va-nu al bi-ur chameitz.

We praise You, Eternal God, Ruler of time and space, for You hallow us with Your Mitzvot, and call us to remove leavened bread from our homes.

After the removal of the leaven the following is recited:

הִנְנוּ מוּכָנִים לְקַבֵּל בְּבֵיתֵנוּ
אֶת־חַג הַמַּצוֹת; יָבֹא
לִקְרָאתֵנוּ לְחֵרוּת וּלְשָׁלוֹם.

Hin'nu muchanim l'kabeil b'veiteinu et chag hamatzot; yavo likrateinu l'cheirut u-l'shalom.

We are now ready to welcome the Festival of Unleavened Bread into our home; may it bring us freedom and peace.

הגדה של פסח

Gates of Freedom:
A Passover Haggadah

For All My Beloved

living in me

and

living with me

פתיחה | Opening

Leader:

Long ago, at this season, a people—our people—set out on a Journey.

On such a night as this, Israel went forth from degradation to joy. We give thanks for the liberations of days gone by.

And we pray for all who are still bound.

Eternal God, may all who hunger come to rejoice in a new Passover.

Let all the human family sit at Your table, drink the wine of deliverance, eat the bread of freedom:

Leader:	**All:**
Freedom from bondage	*and freedom from oppression,*
freedom from hunger	*and freedom from want,*
freedom from hatred	*and freedom from fear,*
freedom to think	*and freedom to speak,*
freedom to teach	*and freedom to learn,*
freedom to love	*and freedom to share,*
freedom to hope	*and freedom to rejoice,*
soon, in our days,	*amen.*

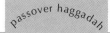
הדלקת הנרות | Kindling the Lights

Leader:

"The people who walked in darkness have seen a great light." From bondage to freedom, from darkness to light: this has been the path of our life; for this we give thanks:

All:

בָּרוּךְ אַתָּה יי אֱלֹהֵינוּ מֶלֶךְ הָעוֹלָם, אֲשֶׁר קִדְּשָׁנוּ בְּמִצְוֹתָיו וְצִוָּנוּ לְהַדְלִיק נֵר שֶׁל (שַׁבָּת וְשֶׁל) יוֹם טוֹב.

Ba-ruch a-ta Adonai, Eh-lo-hei-nu meh-lech ha-o-lam, a-sher ki-d'sha-nu b'mitz-vo-tav v'tzi-va-nu l'had-lik neir shel (Shabbat v'shel) Yom Tov.

p. 94

We praise You, Eternal One: You call us to holiness, and enjoin us to kindle (the Sabbath and) Festival lights.

All:

בָּרוּךְ אַתָּה יי אֱלֹהֵינוּ מֶלֶךְ הָעוֹלָם, שֶׁהֶחֱיָנוּ וְקִיְּמָנוּ וְהִגִּיעָנוּ לַזְּמַן הַזֶּה.

Ba-ruch a-ta Adonai, Eh-lo-hei-nu meh-lech ha-o-lam, she-heh-cheh-ya-nu, v'ki-y'ma nu, v'hi-gi-a-nu la-z'man ha-zeh.

We praise You, Eternal One, for keeping us in life, for sustaining us, and for enabling us to reach this season.

Light is the great metaphor of the spirit's quest and of its satisfaction, as it is said: "By Your light we shall see light." We journey toward the Land of Promise accompanied by the light of the Shechinah, the Divine Presence, our inner light.

Leader:

For all of us, and especially for the children, who will in their turn be keepers of the flame, we ask God's blessing:

יְבָרֶכְךָ יהוה וְיִשְׁמְרֶךָ.

יָאֵר יהוה פָּנָיו אֵלֶיךָ וִיחֻנֶּךָ.

יִשָּׂא יהוה פָּנָיו אֵלֶיךָ וְיָשֵׂם לְךָ שָׁלוֹם.

Y'va-reh-ch'cha Adonai v'yishm'reh-cha.
Ya-er Adonai pa-nav ei-leh-cha vi-chu-neh-ka.
Yi-sa Adonai pa-nav ei-leh-cha
v'ya-seim l'cha shalom.

May God bless you and keep you. May God look kindly upon you, and be gracious to you. May God reach out to You in tenderness, and give you peace.

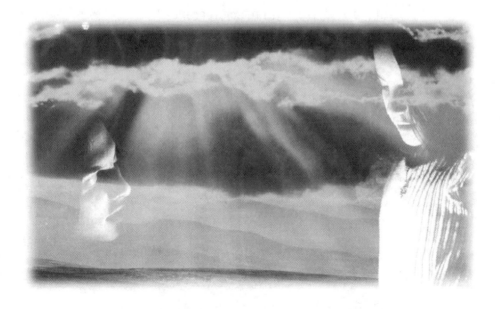

קדש | Kadesh
The cups are filled

Leader:

Tonight we drink four cups of wine. There are many explanations for this custom. They represent, some have said,

- the "four corners of the earth," for freedom must reign everywhere;

- the four seasons of the year, for freedom must be guarded at all times;

- the "four empires" that oppressed us in days of old, for tyranny must pass away as did these empires, before all the world is free.

- Above all, they stand for the four promises of redemption recorded in the story of the liberation of our people from Egyptian bondage (Exodus 6:6-7):

All:

I WILL BRING YOU OUT

I WILL DELIVER YOU

I WILL REDEEM YOU

I WILL TAKE YOU TO BE MY PEOPLE

We will drink four times in this Seder, in remembrance of the four promises of liberation. The first represents our liberation from physical bondage. Until we get out of Egypt we are not free. Only then can we rest on Shabbat— a reminder of the Exodus—and celebrate Pesach, festival of our liberation.

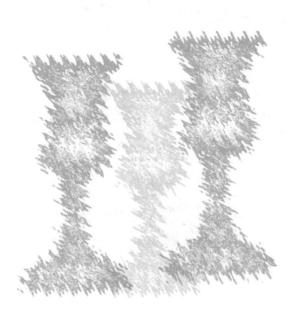

כוס של קדוש | The first cup

Leader:

We raise our cups in remembrance of the beginning of our redemption, as it is said:

All:

אֲנִי יהוה, וְהוֹצֵאתִי אֶתְכֶם
מִתַּחַת סִבְלֹת מִצְרָיִם

A-ni Adonai, V'HO-TZEI-TI
et-chem mi-ta-chat siv-lot
Mitz-ra-yim.

I am the Eternal One, and I will BRING YOU OUT from under the Egyptian yoke.

For Shabbat only:

וַיְהִי־עֶרֶב וַיְהִי־בֹקֶר יוֹם הַשִּׁשִּׁי. וַיְכֻלּוּ הַשָּׁמַיִם וְהָאָרֶץ
וְכָל־צְבָאָם: וַיְכַל אֱלֹהִים בַּיּוֹם הַשְּׁבִיעִי מְלַאכְתּוֹ אֲשֶׁר
עָשָׂה: וַיִּשְׁבֹּת בַּיּוֹם הַשְּׁבִיעִי מִכָּל־מְלַאכְתּוֹ אֲשֶׁר עָשָׂה:
וַיְבָרֶךְ אֱלֹהִים אֶת־יוֹם הַשְּׁבִיעִי וַיְקַדֵּשׁ אֹתוֹ כִּי בוֹ
שָׁבַת מִכָּל־מְלַאכְתּוֹ אֲשֶׁר־בָּרָא אֱלֹהִים לַעֲשׂוֹת:

Va-y'hi eh-rev va-y'hi vo-ker, yom ha-shi-shi. Va-y'chu-lu ha-sha-ma-yim v'ha-a-retz v'chol tz'va-am, va-y'chal Eh-lo-him ba-yom ha-sh'vi-i m'lach-to a-sher a-sa, va-yish-bot ba-yom ha-sh'vi-i mi-kol m'lach-to a-sher a-sa. Va-y'va-rech E-lo-him et yom ha-sh'vi-i va-y'ka-deish o-to, ki vo sha-vat mi-kol m' lach-to a-sher ba-ra E-lo-him la-a-sot.

And God, having completed the work of creation, rested from all that work. God then blessed the seventh day and called it holy, for on it God had completed creation's work.

בָּרוּךְ אַתָּה יי אֱלֹהֵינוּ מֶלֶךְ הָעוֹלָם, בּוֹרֵא פְּרִי הַגָּפֶן.

בָּרוּךְ אַתָּה יי אֱלֹהֵינוּ מֶלֶךְ הָעוֹלָם, אֲשֶׁר בָּחַר בָּנוּ מִכָּל־עָם, וְרוֹמְמָנוּ מִכָּל־לָשׁוֹן, וְקִדְּשָׁנוּ בְּמִצְוֹתָיו.

וַתִּתֶּן לָנוּ, יי אֱלֹהֵינוּ, בְּאַהֲבָה (שַׁבָּתוֹת לִמְנוּחָה וּ) מוֹעֲדִים לְשִׂמְחָה, חַגִּים וּזְמַנִּים לְשָׂשׂוֹן אֶת־יוֹם (הַשַּׁבָּת הַזֶּה וְאֶת־יוֹם) חַג הַמַּצּוֹת הַזֶּה, זְמַן חֵרוּתֵנוּ, (בְּאַהֲבָה) מִקְרָא קֹדֶשׁ, זֵכֶר לִיצִיאַת מִצְרָיִם. כִּי־בָנוּ בָחַרְתָּ וְאוֹתָנוּ קִדַּשְׁתָּ מִכָּל־הָעַמִּים, (וְשַׁבָּת) וּמוֹעֲדֵי קָדְשֶׁךָ (בְּאַהֲבָה וּבְרָצוֹן,) בְּשִׂמְחָה וּבְשָׂשׂוֹן הִנְחַלְתָּנוּ.

בָּרוּךְ אַתָּה יי מְקַדֵּשׁ (הַשַּׁבָּת וְ) יִשְׂרָאֵל וְהַזְּמַנִּים.

Ba-ruch a-ta Adonai, Eh-lo-hei-nu meh-lech ha-o-lam, bo-rei p'ri ha-ga-fen.

Ba-ruch a-ta Adonai, Eh-lo-hei-nu meh-lech ha-o-lam, a-sher ba-char ba-nu mi-kol am, v'ro-m'ma-nu mi-kol la-shon, v'kid'sha-nu b'mitz-vo-tav.

Va-ti-ten la-nu, Adonai Eh-lohei-nu, b'a-ha-va [sha-ba-tot li-m'nu-cha u-] mo-a-dim l'sim-cha, cha-gim u-z'ma-nim l'sa-son, et yom [ha-sha-bat ha-zeh v'et yom] chag ha-ma-tzot ha-zeh-z'man chei-ru-tei-nu, mik-ra ko-desh, zei-cher li-tzi-at mitz-ra-yim.

Ki va-nu v'char-ta v'o-ta-nu ki-dash-ta mi-kol ha-a-mim, [v'sha-bat u-] mo-a-dei kod-sh'cha [b'a-ha-va u-v'ra-tzon,] b'sim-cha u-v'sa-son hin-chal-ta-nu.

Ba-ruch a-ta Adonai, m'ka-deish [ha-sha-bat v'] Yis-ra-eil v'ha-z'ma-nim.

We praise You, Eternal One, for the fruit of the vine.

Eternal God, You call us to Your service and hallow us with Mitzvot. In Your love You have given us the Sabbath and its rest, festive times and seasons, and their joys. They are sacred meeting-days, reminders of our liberation from Egyptian bondage.

We praise You, Eternal One, for these days sacred to Israel.

On Saturday night, continue with Havdalah.

הבדלה | Havdalah

On Saturday night all look at the Festival lights and say:

All:

בָּרוּךְ אַתָּה יי אֱלֹהֵינוּ מֶלֶךְ
הָעוֹלָם, בּוֹרֵא מְאוֹרֵי הָאֵשׁ.

Ba-ruch a-ta Adonai, Eh-lo-hei-nu meh-lech ha-o-lam, bo-rei m'o-rei ha-eish.

We praise You, Eternal One, Creator of the light of fire.

בָּרוּךְ אַתָּה יי אֱלֹהֵינוּ מֶלֶךְ הָעוֹלָם, הַמַּבְדִּיל בֵּין קֹדֶשׁ
לְחוֹל, בֵּין אוֹר לְחֹשֶׁךְ, בֵּין יִשְׂרָאֵל לָעַמִּים, בֵּין יוֹם
הַשְּׁבִיעִי לְשֵׁשֶׁת יְמֵי הַמַּעֲשֶׂה. בֵּין קְדֻשַּׁת שַׁבָּת לִקְדֻשַּׁת
יוֹם טוֹב הִבְדַּלְתָּ וְאֶת־יוֹם הַשְּׁבִיעִי מִשֵּׁשֶׁת יְמֵי הַמַּעֲשֶׂה
קִדַּשְׁתָּ; הִבְדַּלְתָּ וְקִדַּשְׁתָּ אֶת־עַמְּךָ יִשְׂרָאֵל בִּקְדֻשָּׁתֶךָ.
בָּרוּךְ אַתָּה יי הַמַּבְדִּיל בֵּין קֹדֶשׁ לְקֹדֶשׁ.

Ba-ruch a-ta Adonai, Eh-lo-hei-nu meh-lech ha-o-lam, ha-mav-dil bein ko-desh l'chol, bein or l'cho-shech, bein Yis-ra-el la-a-mim, bein yom ha-sh'vi'i l'shei-shet y'mei ha-ma-a-seh. Bein k'du-shat Shabbat li-k'du-shat Yom Tov hiv-dal-ta v'et yom ha-sh'vi'i mi-shei-shet y'mei ha-ma-aseh ki-dash-ta; hiv-dal-ta v'ki-dash-ta et a-m'cha Yis-ra-el bi-k'du-sha-teh-cha. Ba-ruch a-ta Adonai, ha-mav-dil bein ko-desh l'ko-desh.

We praise You, Eternal One: You make distinctions, teaching us to distinguish the commonplace from the holy; You create light and darkness, Israel and the nations, the seventh day of rest and the six days of labor. And you have given each sacred day its own holiness, dividing Sabbath from Festival. For all this, we praise You, O God.

בָּרוּךְ אַתָּה יי אֱלֹהֵינוּ מֶלֶךְ
הָעוֹלָם, שֶׁהֶחֱיָנוּ וְקִיְּמָנוּ
וְהִגִּיעָנוּ לַזְּמַן הַזֶּה.

Ba-ruch a-ta Adonai, Eh-lo-hei-nu meh-lech ha-o-lam, she-heh-cheh-ya-nu, v'ki-y'ma-nu, v'hi-gi-a-nu la-z'man ha-zeh.

We praise You, Eternal One, for keeping us in life, for sustaining us, and for enabling us to reach this season.

All now drink the first cup

כרפס | Karpas

A Reader:

"Spring hangs her infant blossoms on the trees,
Rock'd in the cradle of the western breeze."
When earth is freed from winter's yoke,
When lambs are born and trees turn green,
We celebrate the renewal of life and growth, of hope and love.

Leader:

קוּמִי לָךְ רַעְיָתִי,
יָפָתִי וּלְכִי־לָךְ!
כִּי־הִנֵּה הַסְּתָו עָבָר,
הַגֶּשֶׁם חָלַף הָלַךְ לוֹ.
הַנִּצָּנִים נִרְאוּ בָאָרֶץ,
עֵת הַזָּמִיר הִגִּיעַ.
וְקוֹל הַתּוֹר נִשְׁמַע בְּאַרְצֵנוּ.

Rise up, my love,
my fair one, and come away!
For now the winter is past,
the rains are over and gone.
The flowers appear on the earth,
the time of singing has come.
The song of the dove is heard in
  our land.

All:

רְאֵה קָמָה לְמַלֵּאת,
בִּרְסִיסֵי בְרָכָה:
לֶחֶם לָאוֹכֵל,
וּמַרְפֵּא וַאֲרוּכָה.
לְמַלְבִּישׁ סוּת סְמָדָר
עֲרוּמֵי שׂוֹרֵקָה;
וְהַשָּׁמַיִם יִתְּנוּ טַלָּם.

The standing corn grows ripe,
as dew-drops bring their blessing:
food for the hungry,
healing for the sick.
The grapevines blossom,
as the heavens yield their dew.

The green herbs are dipped in salt water

All:

בָּרוּךְ אַתָּה יי אֱלֹהֵינוּ מֶלֶךְ
הָעוֹלָם, בּוֹרֵא פְּרִי הָאֲדָמָה.

Ba-ruch a-ta Adonai, Eh-lo-hei-nu
meh-lech ha-o-lam, bo-rei p'ri
ha-a-da-mah.

We praise You, Eternal One, Creator of the fruit of the earth.

The green herbs are eaten

יחץ | **Breaking the Matzah**

One of the company takes out the middle Matzah and breaks it in two. The larger piece, known as the Afikoman, will presently be hidden away either by the leader or by the children. The smaller piece is replaced between the two whole Matzot, which are raised while the following is recited:

All:

p. 95

As we eat the "bread of affliction," we reflect that we are not alone. In the Hebrew root that means "affliction" we also find the word "answers." The answer to our afflictions begins to come when we embrace others who are afflicted. "Come share our Passover."

הָא לַחְמָא עַנְיָא,   *Ha lach-ma an-ya*

דִּי אֲכָלוּ אַבְהָתָנָא   *di a-cha-lu a-va-ha-ta-na*

בְּאַרְעָא דְמִצְרָיִם.   *b'ar'a d'mitz-ra-yim.*

כָּל־דִּכְפִין יֵיתֵי וְיֵכֻל,   *kol dich-fin yei-tei v'yei-chul,*

כָּל־דִּצְרִיךְ יֵיתֵי וְיִפְסַח.   *kol ditz-rich yei-tei v'yif-sach.*

הָשַׁתָּא הָכָא,   *Ha-sha-ta ha-cha,*

לַשָּׁנָה הַבָּאָה בְּאַרְעָא   *la-sha-na ha-ba'a*

דְיִשְׂרָאֵל.   *b'ar'a d'yis-ra'el.*

הָשַׁתָּא עַבְדֵי,   *Ha-sha-ta av-dei,*

לַשָּׁנָה הַבָּאָה   *la-sha-na ha-ba'a b'nei cho-rin.*

בְּנֵי חוֹרִין.

This is the bread of affliction our ancestors ate
in the land of Egypt.
Let all who are hungry come and eat;
Let all who are in need come share our Passover.
This year here,
next year in Israel;
today bound,
tomorrow free.

A fourth Matzah may be set aside for all who are separated from us against their will: the afflicted, the oppressed, the unfree, the prisoners of conscience.

The cups are refilled

One or more of the following might now be recited:

Rabbi Bunam said: At the Seder we eat the Matzah first and the Bitter Herbs next, though the reverse order would seem more appropriate, since we first suffered and later went free. There is a reason for this. As long as they had no hope of redemption, they did not feel the real bitterness of their lot. But as soon as Moses spoke to them of freedom, they awoke to the bitterness of their slavery.

—*Chasidic*

There are people in the world so hungry that God cannot appear to them except in the form of bread (After M.K. Gandhi)

The Symbols

מוֹצִיא מַצָה-מָרוֹר-כּוֹרֵךְ MOTZI MATZAH-MAROR-KORECH

Leader:

רַבָּן גַּמְלִיאֵל הָיָה אוֹמֵר: כָּל־שֶׁלֹּא אָמַר שְׁלֹשָׁה דְבָרִים אֵלּוּ בַּפֶּסַח לֹא יָצָא יְדֵי חוֹבָתוֹ. וְאֵלּוּ הֵן: פֶּסַח מַצָה וּמָרוֹר.

Rabban Gamaliel used to say: If, on Passover, you do not explain these three things, you have not fulfilled your obligation:

- Pesach, the paschal lamb;
- Matzah, the unleavened bread;
- and Maror, the bitter herbs.

A Reader:

פֶּסַח שֶׁהָיוּ אֲבוֹתֵינוּ וְאִמּוֹתֵינוּ אוֹכְלִין בִּזְמַן שֶׁבֵּית הַמִּקְדָּשׁ קַיָּם: עַל שׁוּם מַה?

Pesach: Why did our ancestors eat the Passover offering when the Temple still stood?

A Reader:

עַל שׁוּם שֶׁפֶּסַח הַקָּדוֹשׁ בָּרוּךְ הוּא עַל בָּתֵּי אֲבוֹתֵינוּ וְאִמּוֹתֵינוּ בְּמִצְרָיִם, שֶׁנֶּאֱמַר: וַאֲמַרְתֶּם, זֶבַח־פֶּסַח הוּא לַיהוה, אֲשֶׁר פָּסַח עַל־בָּתֵּי בְנֵי־יִשְׂרָאֵל בְּמִצְרַיִם בְּנָגְפּוֹ אֶת־מִצְרַיִם, וְאֶת־בָּתֵּינוּ הִצִּיל.

Because the Holy One passed over the houses of our ancestors in Egypt. As it is said: "It is a Passover offering to the Eternal One, who passed over the houses of the people of Israel when Egypt was smitten; but our houses were spared."

A reader holds up the shank-bone and says:

"When the Temple still stood"—nearly two thousand years have passed since that time. But this night past and present merge, and we remember our beginnings. This bone helps us recall the paschal lamb our ancestors offered long ago.

A reader holds up the roasted egg and says:

This egg reminds us of the Festival Offering through which the priests, in Temple days, expressed their prayer for the well-being of the people. It is also a sign of rebirth. As all around us nature dances with new life, so may this season stir within us new strength, new hope, new joy.

Leader

מַצָּה זוּ שֶׁאָנוּ אוֹכְלִים: Matzah:
עַל שׁוּם מַה? Why do we eat it?

A Reader:

עַל שׁוּם שֶׁלֹא הִסְפִּיק בְּצֵקָם שֶׁל אֲבוֹתֵינוּ וְאִמוֹתֵינוּ
לְהַחֲמִיץ, עַד שֶׁנִּגְלָה עֲלֵיהֶם מֶלֶךְ מַלְכֵי הַמְּלָכִים, הַקָּדוֹשׁ
בָּרוּךְ הוּא, וּגְאָלָם, שֶׁנֶּאֱמַר: וַיֹּאפוּ אֶת־הַבָּצֵק אֲשֶׁר הוֹצִיאוּ
מִמִּצְרַיִם עֻגֹת מַצּוֹת, כִּי לֹא חָמֵץ, כִּי־גֹרְשׁוּ מִמִּצְרַיִם וְלֹא
יָכְלוּ לְהִתְמַהְמֵהַּ, וְגַם־צֵדָה לֹא־עָשׂוּ לָהֶם.

Because the Holy One stood revealed before our ancestors to redeem them, even before their dough had time to ferment. As it is said: "They baked the dough they had brought out of Egypt into unleavened cakes, for they were driven out of Egypt without being given time to prepare food."

A Reader:

Free Romans at their banquets would recline on couches, leaning to the left, to leave their right hands unencumbered, while slaves attended them. Now we re-enact that scene, without slaves, to celebrate the fall of slavemasters who thought their rule would last forever. So leaning is a way of rejoicing in liberation, and a symbol of our hope that before long, all the families, tribes, and peoples of the earth will eat and drink at freedom's banquet.

One of the company raises the Matzah plate, and all say:

בָּרוּךְ אַתָּה יי אֱלֹהֵינוּ מֶלֶךְ הָעוֹלָם הַמּוֹצִיא לֶחֶם מִן הָאָרֶץ.

Ba-ruch a-ta Adonai, Eh-lo-hei-nu meh-lech ha-o-lam, ha-mo-tzi le-chem min ha-a-retz.

בָּרוּךְ אַתָּה יי אֱלֹהֵינוּ מֶלֶךְ הָעוֹלָם אֲשֶׁר קִדְּשָׁנוּ בְּמִצְוֹתָיו וְצִוָּנוּ עַל אֲכִילַת מַצָּה.

Ba-ruch a-ta Adonai, Eh-lo-hei-nu me-lech ha-o-lam, a-sher kid'sha-nu b'mitz-vo-tav v'tzi-va-nu al a-chi-lat Mat-zah.

We praise You, Eternal One, for the bread that comes from the earth. We praise You, Eternal One, for the Mitzvah of eating unleavened bread.

All lean to the left and eat a piece of Matzah, the leader breaking a piece from the upper Matzah and another from the remainder of the middle one, and eating them together.

Leader:

מָרוֹר זֶה שֶׁאָנוּ אוֹכְלִים: עַל שׁוּם מַה?

Maror: Why do we eat it?

A Reader:

עַל שׁוּם שֶׁמֵּרְרוּ הַמִּצְרִים אֶת־חַיֵּי אֲבוֹתֵינוּ וְאִמּוֹתֵינוּ בְּמִצְרַיִם, שֶׁנֶּאֱמַר: וַיְמָרְרוּ אֶת־חַיֵּיהֶם בַּעֲבֹדָה קָשָׁה, בְּחֹמֶר וּבִלְבֵנִים, וּבְכָל־עֲבֹדָה בַּשָּׂדֶה; אֵת כָּל־עֲבֹדָתָם אֲשֶׁר־עָבְדוּ בָהֶם בְּפָרֶךְ.

Because the Egyptians embittered the lives of our ancestors in Egypt. As it is said: "They made life bitter for them with hard labor at mortar and brick, and with every kind of field work; they drove them in their work with utter ruthlessness."

Leader:

Before eating the Maror, we dip it in Charoset. It looks like the clay and straw with which our people were forced to make bricks for Pharaoh's building projects in Egypt. Its sweet taste softens, but does not remove, the bitter memory of their slavery.

All take a piece of Maror, dip it in Charoset, and say:

בָּרוּךְ אַתָּה יי אֱלֹהֵינוּ מֶלֶךְ
הָעוֹלָם, אֲשֶׁר קִדְּשָׁנוּ
בְּמִצְוֹתָיו וְצִוָּנוּ עַל אֲכִילַת
מָרוֹר.

Ba-ruch a-ta Adonai,
Eh-lo-hei-nu me-lech ha-o-lam,
a-sher kid'sha-nu
b'mitz-vo-tav v'tzi-va-nu al
a-chi-lat ma-ror.

We praise You, Eternal One, for the Mitzvah of eating bitter herbs.

The Maror is eaten

All place another piece of Maror and Charoset between two pieces of Matzah, the leader breaking these from the lower Matzah. All recite:

כֵּן עָשָׂה הִלֵּל בִּזְמַן שֶׁבֵּית הַמִּקְדָּשׁ הָיָה קַיָּם: הָיָה כּוֹרֵךְ
מַצָּה וּמָרוֹר וְאוֹכֵל בְּיַחַד, לְקַיֵּם מַה־שֶׁנֶּאֱמַר: עַל מַצּוֹת
וּמְרֹרִים יֹאכְלֻהוּ.

This was Hillel's practice in the days of the Temple: he would combine (the Passover lamb with) unleavened bread and bitter herbs (Pesach, Matzah, Maror) and eat them together, to fulfill the verse: "They shall eat it with unleavened bread and bitter herbs."

Leader:

We hold the Matzah of freedom, the "mortar" of forced labor, the bitter Maror of bondage. We take into ourselves the joys and sorrows of the ages.

All now eat the "Hillel Sandwich."

p. 96

ארבע קשיות | The Four Questions

To be asked by the youngest person(s) present

מַה־נִּשְׁתַּנָּה הַלַּיְלָה הַזֶּה   *Ma nish-ta-na ha-lai-la ha-zeh*

מִכָּל־הַלֵּילוֹת?   *mi-kol ha-lai-lot?*

שֶׁבְּכָל־הַלֵּילוֹת   *Sheh-b'chol ha-lei-lot*

אָנוּ אוֹכְלִין חָמֵץ וּמַצָּה,   *a-nu o-ch'lin cha-meitz u-matzah,*

הַלַּיְלָה הַזֶּה כֻּלּוֹ מַצָּה.   *ha-lai-la ha-zeh ku-lo matzah.*

שֶׁבְּכָל־הַלֵּילוֹת   *Sheh-b'chol ha-lei-lot*

אָנוּ אוֹכְלִין שְׁאָר יְרָקוֹת,   *anu och'lin sh'ar y'ra-kot,*

הַלַּיְלָה הַזֶּה מָרוֹר.   *ha-lai-la ha-zeh ma-ror.*

שֶׁבְּכָל־הַלֵּילוֹת   *Sheh-b'chol ha-lei-lot*

אֵין אָנוּ מַטְבִּילִין   *ein a-nu mat-bi-lin*

אֲפִלּוּ פַּעַם אֶחָת,   *a-fi-lu pa-am eh-chat,*

הַלַּיְלָה הַזֶּה שְׁתֵּי פְעָמִים.   *ha-lai-la ha-zeh sh'tei f'a-mim.*

שֶׁבְּכָל־הַלֵּילוֹת   *Sheh-b'chol ha-lei-lot*

אָנוּ אוֹכְלִין בֵּין יוֹשְׁבִין   *a-nu o-ch'lin bein yo-sh'vin*

וּבֵין מְסֻבִּין,   *u-vein m'su-bin,*

הַלַּיְלָה הַזֶּה כֻּלָּנוּ מְסֻבִּין.   *ha-lai-la ha-zeh ku-la-nu m'su-bin.*

Every journey to freedom is a journey of the spirit; every journey of the spirit begins with a question; and of all questions, deepest is this: Why? Asking leads to liberation, and the right to ask is the primary means to the liberation of mind and soul. The ability to question is a precious gift: this parents must nurture within their children.

Why is this night different from all other nights?

On other nights we eat bread leavened or unleavened:
on this night, unleavened only!

On other nights we eat all kinds of herbs:
on this night, bitter herbs!

On other nights we do not dip herbs at all:
on this night, twice!

On other nights we eat sitting upright or leaning:
on this night, we all lean!

All:

*You are free to ask,
you are free to question,
free to learn the answers of tradition,
free to add answers of your own!*

ארבע בנות/ארבעה בנים | The Four Children

A Reader:

מִשְׁאֵלָתוֹ | The questions children ask,

וּמִדִּבּוּרוֹ | the way they speak,

אַתָּה יוֹדֵעַ מַה־דַּעְתּוֹ. | will tell you what they are like.

וּלְפִי דַעְתּוֹ שֶׁל הַבֵּן | And parents should teach them

אָבִיו מְלַמְּדוֹ. | according to their particular natures.

A Reader:

כְּנֶגֶד אַרְבָּעָה בָנִים | The Torah speaks of four types of
דִּבְּרָה תוֹרָה: | persons:

- אֶחָד חָכָם | • the wise,
- וְאֶחָד רָשָׁע | • the wicked,
- וְאֶחָד תָּם | • the simple,
- וְאֶחָד שֶׁאֵינוֹ יוֹדֵעַ לִשְׁאוֹל. | • the one who does not know enough to ask.

You cannot be redeemed until you see your own flaws, and try to correct them. We can be redeemed only to the extent to which we see ourselves. —*Chasidic*

Even in the lowliest of human beings there dwells a soul, a sacred mystery, the garment of the living God. This garment we must keep spotless and return it without blemish. How? Through purity of heart, clarity of mind, and love for all creatures. —*Chasidic/cs*

Leader:

חָכָם מַה הוּא אוֹמֵר?   What does the wise one say?

A Reader:

מַה הָעֵדֹת וְהַחֻקִּים וְהַמִּשְׁפָּטִים אֲשֶׁר צִוָּה יהוה אֱלֹהֵינוּ אֹתָנוּ? וְאַף אַתָּה אֱמָר לוֹ כְּהִלְכוֹת הַפֶּסַח: אֵין מַפְטִירִין אַחַר הַפֶּסַח אֲפִיקוֹמָן.

This one says: "What are the duties, laws and rules that our God has taught us?" Such questioners should be encouraged to learn all the lessons of Pesach from beginning to end. They will become our teachers.

Leader:

רָשָׁע מַה הוּא אוֹמֵר?   What do the wicked say?

A Reader:

מַה הָעֲבוֹדָה הַזֹּאת לָכֶם?
לָכֶם וְלֹא לוֹ. וּלְפִי שֶׁהוֹצִיא אֶת־עַצְמוֹ מִן הַכְּלָל וְכָפַר בָּעִקָּר, אַף אַתָּה הַקְהֵה אֶת־שִׁנָּיו וֶאֱמָר לוֹ: בַּעֲבוּר זֶה עָשָׂה יי לִי בְּצֵאתִי מִמִּצְרָיִם.

The Koretzer Rebbe said: Within us are all the worlds, and we can therefore be in contact with them all. Within us are all the qualities, good and evil, but they are unborn, and we have the power to beget them. We can transform evil qualities into good, and good into evil. By learning Torah and doing Mitzvot we give birth to the angelic within us. —*Chasidic*

They say: "What is this service to you?"

To *you* and not to *us!* And since (by doing this) they cut themselves off from the community and scorn our faith, make this sharp retort, telling them: "I do this because of what the Eternal did for me when I came out of Egypt."

A Reader:

לִי וְלֹא לוֹ:   For *me* and not for *them.*
אִלוּ הָיָה שָׁם   Had they been there,
לֹא הָיָה נִגְאָל.   they would have denied their own need of redemption.

A Reader:

הִלֵּל אוֹמֵר: אַל־תִּפְרוֹשׁ מִן־הַצִּבּוּר.

Hillel said: Do not separate yourself from the community.

A Reader:

הוּא הָיָה אוֹמֵר: אִם אֵין אֲנִי לִי, מִי לִי?
וּכְשֶׁאֲנִי לְעַצְמִי מָה אֲנִי? וְאִם לֹא עַכְשָׁו אֵימָתָי?

He used to say: If I am not for myself, who will be for me? But if I
am only for myself, what am I? And if not now, when?

A Reader:

Will you seek far off? You surely come back at last, in things
best known to you, finding the best, or as good as the best—

All:

*Happiness, knowledge, not in another place, but in this place—
not for another hour, but this hour. (Walt Whitman)*

Leader:

תָּם מַה הוּא אוֹמֵר? What does the simple one say?

A Reader:

מַה־זֹּאת?

וְאָמַרְתָּ אֵלָיו: בְּחֹזֶק יָד הוֹצִיאָנוּ יי מִמִּצְרַיִם מִבֵּית עֲבָדִים.

"What is this?"
To this one tell the story of our liberation, saying: "With a
mighty hand God led us out of Egypt, out of the house of bondage."

All:

וְשֶׁאֵינוֹ יוֹדֵעַ לִשְׁאוֹל
אַתְּ פְּתַח לוֹ שֶׁנֶּאֱמַר:
וְהִגַּדְתָּ לְבִנְךָ בַּיּוֹם
הַהוּא . . .

*And with the one who does not
know enough to ask, you must
take the first step. As it is said:
"You shall tell your child on that
day."*

A Reader:

Every one of us contains all four types: we are the one unable to ask, the simple one, the wicked
one, and the wise one. Sometimes we don't even know there is a question: we are then the one who
does not know enough to ask; yet again we are the one who asks an innocent question and is
satisfied by a "simple" answer: we don't think to look beneath the surface. And within us, as well,
is the "wicked" one, alienated, estranged, wondering why we are part of all this, wanting to go on a
different path. But we are wise, too, sometimes: wise enough to ask, not once but repeatedly, humbly
but passionately seeking truth invisible to the naked eye, well aware that answers beget questions,
but feeling, too, the privilege that belongs to a community that values the liberty of the seeker.

On the side of the road
there are leaves
so tired of being leaves
they have fallen.
On the side of the road
there are Jews
so tired of being Jews
they have fallen.
Sweep away the leaves.
Sweep away the Jews.
The same leaves, will they
grow again in spring?
Will there be a spring
for the downtrodden
Jews? —*Edmond Jabès*

מגיד | The Narration

Questions call for answers. In answer we tell our story again and again, and we linger over the details.

A Reader:

מַתְחִיל (לְהַגִּיד) בִּגְנוּת; וּמְסַיֵּם (לְסַפֵּר) בְּשֶׁבַח.

Our story begins with degradation; our telling ends with glory.

All:

עֲבָדִים הָיִינוּ לְפַרְעֹה בְּמִצְרָיִם. וַיּוֹצִיאֵנוּ יי אֱלֹהֵינוּ מִשָּׁם בְּיָד חֲזָקָה וּבִזְרֹעַ נְטוּיָה. וְאִלּוּ לֹא הוֹצִיא הַקָּדוֹשׁ בָּרוּךְ הוּא אֶת־אֲבוֹתֵינוּ וְאִמּוֹתֵינוּ מִמִּצְרַיִם, הֲרֵי אָנוּ וּבָנֵינוּ וּבְנֵי בָנֵינוּ מְשֻׁעְבָּדִים הָיִינוּ לְפַרְעֹה בְּמִצְרָיִם.

We were slaves to Pharaoh in Egypt, and our God led us out from there with a mighty hand, with an outstretched arm. Had not the Holy One led our ancestors out of Egypt, we and our children and our children's children would still be enslaved.

If you think you can live without others, you are mistaken; but if you think others cannot live without you, you are even more mistaken. —*Chasidic*

A Reader:

וַאֲפִלּוּ כֻּלָּנוּ חֲכָמִים, כֻּלָּנוּ נְבוֹנִים, כֻּלָּנוּ זְקֵנִים, כֻּלָּנוּ יוֹדְעִים אֶת־הַתּוֹרָה, מִצְוָה עָלֵינוּ לְסַפֵּר בִּיצִיאַת מִצְרָיִם. וְכָל־הַמַּרְבֶּה לְסַפֵּר בִּיצִיאַת מִצְרַיִם הֲרֵי זֶה מְשֻׁבָּח.

Therefore, even if all of us were wise, all discerning; scholars, sages, and learned in Torah: we should still have to tell the story of the Exodus. Praised is the one who lingers over the telling!

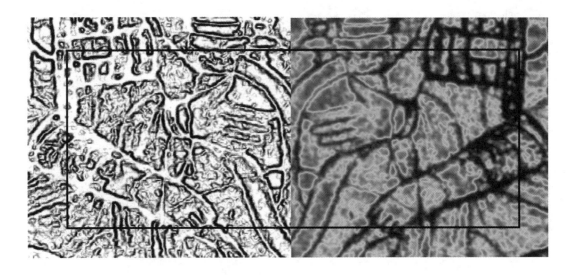

How are we to tell the story of liberation? With passionate absorption! How are we to live as free human beings? With passionate determination! This is what our sages did at a time of Rome's oppressive rule. Were they planning their revolt during their celebration? We cannot be certain. We do know this: One of them, Akiba, led an uprising we still remember. And we note that though these sages had been telling the Pesach story all their lives, they never tired of it: so all that night…

A Reader:

מַעֲשֶׂה בְּרַבִּי אֱלִיעֶזֶר וְרַבִּי יְהוֹשֻׁעַ וְרַבִּי אֶלְעָזָר בֶּן עֲזַרְיָה
וְרַבִּי עֲקִיבָא וְרַבִּי טַרְפוֹן, שֶׁהָיוּ מְסֻבִּין בִּבְנֵי בְרַק, וְהָיוּ
מְסַפְּרִים בִּיצִיאַת מִצְרַיִם כָּל-אוֹתוֹ הַלַּיְלָה, עַד שֶׁבָּאוּ
תַלְמִידֵיהֶם וְאָמְרוּ לָהֶם: רַבּוֹתֵינוּ, הִגִּיעַ זְמַן קְרִיאַת שְׁמַע
שֶׁל שַׁחֲרִית!

They say that Rabbi Eliezer, Rabbi Joshua, Rabbi Elazar ben Azariah, Rabbi Akiba, and Rabbi Tarfon were sitting at the Seder table in B'nei B'rak; all that night they talked about the Exodus, until their students came and said to them: "Rabbis, it is time to recite the morning Shema!"

I can feel the suffering of millions
and yet, if I look up into the heavens,
I think that it will all come right,
that this cruelty too will end,
and that peace and tranquillity will return again.
In the meantime,
I must uphold my ideals,
for perhaps the time will come
when I shall be able to carry them out.
　　　　　　　　　　　—Anne Frank

A Reader:

אָמַר רבִּי אֶלְעָזָר בֶּן עֲזַרְיָה: הֲרֵי אֲנִי כְּבֶן שִׁבְעִים שָׁנָה
וְלֹא זָכִיתִי שֶׁתֵּאָמֵר יְצִיאַת מִצְרַיִם בַּלֵּילוֹת עַד שֶׁדְּרָשָׁהּ
בֶּן זוֹמָא. שֶׁנֶּאֱמַר: לְמַעַן תִּזְכֹּר אֶת־יוֹם צֵאתְךָ מֵאֶרֶץ מִצְרַיִם
כֹּל יְמֵי חַיֶּיךָ. יְמֵי חַיֶּיךָ: הַיָּמִים. כֹּל יְמֵי חַיֶּיךָ: הַלֵּילוֹת.
וַחֲכָמִים אוֹמְרִים: יְמֵי חַיֶּיךָ: הַיָּמִים. כֹּל יְמֵי חַיֶּיךָ: לְהָבִיא
יְמוֹת הַמָּשִׁיחַ.

Rabbi Elazar ben Azariah said: I seem like a man of seventy, yet I never understood why we must tell of the Exodus at night until Ben Zoma came along with this teaching: "Remember the day you went out of Egypt all the days of your life" (Deuteronomy 16:3). It is easy to remember your liberation when the sun is shining. But you must remember it "*all* the days of your life" even when the sun has set, even when your day is dark.

The sages saw an additional lesson in this verse: "The days of your life" are your days in this world—the world as it is; "*all* the days of your life" includes the messianic day. Let our remembrance of liberation help us change the world as it is into the world as it ought to be.

All:

And then all that has divided us will merge
And then compassion will be wedded to power
And then softness will come to a world that is harsh and unkind
And then both men and women will be gentle
And then both women and men will be strong
And then no person will be subject to another's will
And then all will be rich and free and varied
And then the greed of some will give way to the needs of many
And then all will share equally in the earth's abundance
And then all will care for the sick and the weak and the old
And then all will nourish the young
And then all will cherish life's creatures
And then all will live in harmony with each other and Earth
And then everywhere will be called Eden once again.
                                             —Judy Chicago

A Reader:

מַתְחִיל (לְהַגִּיד) בִּגְנוּת;
וּמְסַיֵּם (לְסַפֵּר) בְּשֶׁבַח.

Our story begins with degradation;
our telling ends with glory.

A Reader:

מִתְּחִלָּה עוֹבְדֵי עֲבוֹדָה זָרָה הָיוּ אֲבוֹתֵינוּ; וְעַכְשָׁו קֵרְבָנוּ
הַמָּקוֹם לַעֲבוֹדָתוֹ, שֶׁנֶּאֱמַר: וַיֹּאמֶר יְהוֹשֻׁעַ אֶל־כָּל־הָעָם:
כֹּה־אָמַר יהוה אֱלֹהֵי יִשְׂרָאֵל: בְּעֵבֶר הַנָּהָר יָשְׁבוּ אֲבוֹתֵיכֶם
מֵעוֹלָם: תֶּרַח אֲבִי אַבְרָהָם וַאֲבִי נָחוֹר. וַיַּעַבְדוּ אֱלֹהִים
אֲחֵרִים. וָאֶקַּח אֶת־אֲבִיכֶם, אֶת־אַבְרָהָם, מֵעֵבֶר הַנָּהָר,
וָאוֹלֵךְ אוֹתוֹ בְּכָל־אֶרֶץ כְּנַעַן, וָאַרְבֶּה אֶת־זַרְעוֹ ... וָאֶתֵּן
לְעֵשָׂו אֶת־הַר שֵׂעִיר לָרֶשֶׁת אוֹתוֹ, וְיַעֲקֹב וּבָנָיו יָרְדוּ
מִצְרָיִם.

In the beginning our ancestors served idols; now we are called to
serve the Divine. As it is said: "Thus says the Eternal One, the
God of Israel, Long ago your ancestors lived beyond the River
Euphrates and served other gods. Then I took Abraham and Sarah
from beyond the River, and led them all over the land of Canaan.
I multiplied their descendants... and let Esau take possession of
Mount Seir. But Jacob and his children went down to Egypt."

Leader:

מַתְחִיל (לְהַגִּיד) בִּגְנוּת;
וּמְסַיֵּם (לְסַפֵּר) בְּשֶׁבַח.

Our story begins with degradation;
our telling ends with glory.

All:

אֲרַמִּי אֹבֵד אָבִי.
וַיֵּרֶד מִצְרַיְמָה.
וַיָּגָר שָׁם
בִּמְתֵי מְעָט.
וַיְהִי־שָׁם לְגוֹי גָּדוֹל
עָצוּם וָרָב.
וַיָּרֵעוּ אֹתָנוּ הַמִּצְרִים.
וַיְעַנּוּנוּ.
וַיִּתְּנוּ עָלֵינוּ עֲבֹדָה קָשָׁה.
וַנִּצְעַק אֶל־יהוה
אֱלֹהֵי אֲבֹתֵינוּ.
וַיִּשְׁמַע יהוה אֶת־קֹלֵנוּ,
וַיַּרְא אֶת־עָנְיֵנוּ וְאֶת־עֲמָלֵנוּ,
וְאֶת־לַחֲצֵנוּ.
וַיּוֹצִאֵנוּ יהוה מִמִּצְרַיִם
בְּיָד חֲזָקָה,
וּבִזְרֹעַ נְטוּיָה,
וּבְמֹרָא גָּדוֹל,
וּבְאֹתוֹת וּבְמוֹפְתִים.

Our ancestors were wandering
   Arameans.
They went down to Egypt.
They lived there as strangers,
few in number.
There they became a great nation,
mighty and numerous.
But the Egyptians were cruel to us.
They afflicted us.
They imposed hard labor upon us.
Then we cried out to the Eternal
   One,
the God of our ancestors.
And the Eternal heard our cry,
saw our plight, our woe,
our oppression.
Then God led us out of Egypt
with a mighty hand,
with an outstretched arm,
with awesome power,
with signs and wonders.

There is an enslavement of the spirit; from that Egypt too we must redeem ourselves. We recall our slow difficult rise from the service of idols, and we are not so arrogant or unimginative as to say: "We are rid of them once and for all." Each generation has its idols; every one of us is called to search for truth, to rise above the worship of half-truths and to see material goods for what they are: useful servants, tyrannical rulers.

מדרש | Midrash

יציאת מצרים בפרט | The Exodus In Detail

If you decide to omit this section, continue either with the Alternative Reading that begins on page 36, or on page 42

If you decide to omit this section, continue either with the Alternative Reading that begins on page 36, or on page 42

Leader:

אֲרַמִּי אֹבֵד אָבִי.   "Our ancestors were wandering Arameans."

All:

We began as wanderers, without a home. Again and yet again, we have been wanderers, fugitives, refugees.

Leader:

וַיֵּרֶד מִצְרָיְמָה.   "They went down to Egypt."

A Reader:

Though upon our arrival there we were made welcome in the land of Egypt, in the end our "going down" was a descent into degradation. Not only were we enslaved, but we accepted our lot: when first we heard the divine promise of liberation, we would not listen, "because of our broken spirit."

The real slavery of Israel in Egypt was that they had learned to endure it.
—*Chasidic*

Liberty is not less a blessing, because oppression has so long darkened the mind that it cannot appreciate it.
—*Lucretia Mott*

My very chains and I
grew friends,
So much a long
communion tends
To make us
what we are: even I
Regain'd my freedom
with a sigh.
—*Lord Byron*

Leader:

וַיָּגָר שָׁם בִּמְתֵי מְעָט.

"They lived there as strangers,
few in number."

A Reader:

בְּשִׁבְעִים נֶפֶשׁ יָרְדוּ אֲבֹתֶיךָ מִצְרָיְמָה, וְעַתָּה שָׂמְךָ יהוה
אֱלֹהֶיךָ כְּכוֹכְבֵי הַשָּׁמַיִם לָרֹב.

"Our ancestors who entered Egypt numbered only seventy, and
now our God has made us as numerous as the stars of heaven."

Leader:

וַיְהִי־שָׁם לְגוֹי גָּדוֹל.

"They became a great nation."

A Reader:

וַיְהִי־שָׁם לְגוֹי: מְלַמֵּד
שֶׁהָיוּ יִשְׂרָאֵל מְצֻיָּנִים שָׁם.

The use of the word "nation"
shows that they remained true
to themselves.

Jewish resistance in the concentration camps took many forms. For some, it consisted of a refusal to allow themselves to feel degraded, even in the worst of circumstances. There were Jews who continued to live by Halachah—Jewish Law—even there.

One such Jew addressed a question to Rabbi Ephraim Oshry: "Should a Jew, having to do forced labor for the Nazis, continue to recite the benediction in the morning service, "We praise You, Eternal One, who has not made me a slave"? Rabbi Oshry answered: "Heaven forbid that they should give up reciting the B'rachah that was established by the great sages of yesteryear. On the contrary, now of all times we are obliged to say this B'rachah, so that our adversaries and tormentors realize that, although we are in their power to do with us as their wicked machinations devise, we nonetheless perceive ourselves not as slaves, but as free people, prisoners for the time being, whose liberation will soon come and whose deliverance will quickly be accomplished." —Albert Axelrad

Two women provide us with the first recorded example of spiritual resistance to tyranny. Shifrah and Puah were the midwives ordered by Pharaoh to kill all male children born to Israelite women. "But the midwives feared God and did not do as the King of Egypt had told them, but kept the infants alive." Pharaoh sought to conceal his responsibility for his genocidal plan by acting through the midwives—as though by this means the deaths would appear to be natural. But Shifrah and Puah did not allow him to escape the consequences of his acts. Their moral courage is a model of responsible ethical behavior.

"(They) did not do as the King of Egypt had told them, but kept the infants alive." Strictly speaking the second half of this sentence is superfluous: once we are told that the midwives did not do the bidding of Pharaoh, we know they kept the infants alive. Why then does the Torah add these words? To add to the praise of these women—for keeping them alive means more than not putting them to death. After the birth of these infants, Shifrah and Puah sustained them, bringing food and drink to those who had none by reason of their poverty. (Exodus 1.17, Exodus Rabbah 1.14, Exodus Rabbah 1:15, expanded)

A Reader:

הַצְטַיְנוּתוֹ שֶׁל עַם יִשְׂרָאֵל מַהִי? שְׁלֹשָׁה סִימָנִים יֵשׁ בְּאוּמָה זוֹ: •הָרַחֲמָנִים, •וְהַבַּיְשָׁנִים, •וְגוֹמְלֵי חֲסָדִים.

How did Israel show its
   self-respect?
We have learned:
This people is truly itself when
it displays three virtues:
• compassion,
• modesty,
• and kindness.

Leader:

עָצוּם וָרָב.

"Mighty and numerous."

All:

וּבְנֵי יִשְׂרָאֵל פָּרוּ וַיִּשְׁרְצוּ וַיִּרְבּוּ וַיַּעַצְמוּ בִּמְאֹד מְאֹד, וַתִּמָּלֵא הָאָרֶץ אֹתָם.

The people of Israel were fruitful, their numbers increased rapidly, until the land was full of them.

A Reader:

וַיָּרֵעוּ אֹתָנוּ הַמִּצְרִים.   "But the Egyptians were cruel to us."

A Reader:

שֶׁנֶּאֱמַר: וַיָּקָם מֶלֶךְ־חָדָשׁ עַל־מִצְרָיִם אֲשֶׁר לֹא־יָדַע אֶת־יוֹסֵף. וַיֹּאמֶר אֶל־עַמּוֹ, הִנֵּה עַם בְּנֵי יִשְׂרָאֵל רַב וְעָצוּם מִמֶּנּוּ. הָבָה נִתְחַכְּמָה לוֹ, פֶּן־יִרְבֶּה, וְהָיָה כִּי־תִקְרֶאנָה מִלְחָמָה, וְנוֹסַף גַּם־הוּא עַל־שֹׂנְאֵינוּ, וְנִלְחַם־בָּנוּ וְעָלָה מִן־הָאָרֶץ.

As it is said: "Now a new king rose over Egypt, who 'did not know' Joseph. He said to his people, "Behold, this people Israel is far too numerous for comfort. Let us now deal shrewdly with them, lest they continue to increase and, in the event of war, join our enemies and fight against us, and then escape from the land."

Covey at length let me go, puffing and blowing at a great rate, saying that if I had not resisted, he would not have whipped me half so much. The truth was, that he had not whipped me at all. I considered him as getting entirely the worst end of the bargain; for he had drawn no blood from me, but I had from him. The whole six months afterwards, that I spent with Mr. Covey, he never laid the weight of his finger upon me.

This battle with Mr. Covey was the turning-point of my career as a slave. It rekindled the few expiring embers of freedom, and revived within me a sense of my own manhood.

It was a glorious resurrection, from the tomb of slavery, to the heaven of freedom.
—*Frederick Douglass*

A Reader:

וַיְעַנּוּנוּ.   "They afflicted us."

A Reader:

וַיָּשִׂימוּ עָלָיו שָׂרֵי מִסִּים, לְמַעַן עַנֹּתוֹ בְּסִבְלֹתָם;
וַיִּבֶן עָרֵי מִסְכְּנוֹת לְפַרְעֹה, אֶת־פִּתֹם וְאֶת־רַעַמְסֵס.

As it is said: "They set taskmasters over them, to afflict them
with forced labor; thus they built for Pharaoh store-cities, such as
Pithom and Raamses."

A Reader:

וַיִּתְּנוּ עָלֵינוּ עֲבֹדָה קָשָׁה.   "They imposed hard labor
upon us."

A Reader:

וַיַּעֲבִדוּ מִצְרַיִם אֶת־בְּנֵי יִשְׂרָאֵל בְּפָרֶךְ. שָׁנִינוּ: מְלַמֵּד שֶׁהָיוּ
בְיָדָם מְגִלּוֹת, שֶׁהָיוּ מִשְׁתַּעַשְׁעִין בָּהֶן מִשַּׁבָּת לְשַׁבָּת, לֵאמֹר
שֶׁהַקָּדוֹשׁ בָּרוּךְ הוּא גּוֹאֲלָם, לְפִי שֶׁהָיוּ נוֹחִין בְּשַׁבָּת. אָמַר
לָהֶם פַּרְעֹה: תִּכְבַּד הָעֲבוֹדָה עַל הָאֲנָשִׁים וְיַעֲשׂוּ־בָהּ וְאַל
יִשְׁעוּ בְּדִבְרֵי־שָׁקֶר־אַל יִהְיוּ מִשְׁתַּעַשְׁעִין וְאַל יִהְיוּ נְפֵשִׁים
בְּיוֹם הַשַּׁבָּת.

As it is said: "The Egyptians ruthlessly imposed hard labor upon
the people of Israel." And we have learned: During the bondage,
Israel kept its traditions alive. Each Shabbat their spirits would
revive: the Holy One would redeem them! So Pharaoh decreed:
"Make their work harder; destroy their false hopes"—Let them not
have Sabbaths on which to refresh themselves.

A Reader:

וַנִּצְעַק אֶל־יְהוָה אֱלֹהֵי   "Then we cried out to the
אֲבֹתֵינוּ.   Eternal One, the God of our
ancestors."

A Reader:

וַיְהִי בַיָּמִים הָרַבִּים הָהֵם, וַיָּמָת מֶלֶךְ מִצְרַיִם,
וַיֵּאָנְחוּ בְנֵי־יִשְׂרָאֵל מִן־הָעֲבֹדָה וַיִּזְעָקוּ; וַתַּעַל
שַׁוְעָתָם אֶל־הָאֱלֹהִים מִן־הָעֲבֹדָה.

As it is said: "During those long, painful days, the king of Egypt died. But the people of Israel still groaned under their bondage, and cried out; and the screams wrung from them by their bondage ascended to God."

A Reader:

וַיִּשְׁמַע יהוה אֶת־קֹלֵנוּ.   "And the Eternal heard our cry."

All:

וַיִּשְׁמַע אֱלֹהִים אֶת־נַאֲקָתָם,   As it is said: "God heard their
וַיִּזְכֹּר אֱלֹהִים אֶת־בְּרִיתוֹ...   groans, and God remembered the covenant."

Leader:

And that covenant was made with Abraham and with Sarah, with Isaac and Rebekah, with Jacob, Leah and Rachel, with every member of the House of Israel. It belongs to all ages, all women, all men; it belongs to the children and to the grandparents. It belongs to all of us, even the generations waiting to be born.

A Reader:

וַיַּרְא   "and (the Eternal) saw"

A Reader:

מֶה רָאָה יי? שֶׁהָיוּ מְרַחֲמִים   We have learned: God saw that
זֶה עַל זֶה. כְּשֶׁהָיָה אֶחָד מֵהֶם   the slaves showed compassion for
מַשְׁלִים סְכוּם הַלְּבֵנִים   one another; upon completing
לוֹ קֹדֶם חֲבֵרוֹ הָיָה בָא וּמַסִּיעַ.   their own work-quotas, they would go help the others.

A Reader:

וַיַּרְא . . .
מֶה רָאָה הַקָּדוֹשׁ בָּרוּךְ הוּא?

"and the Eternal saw..."
What did the Holy One see?

A Reader:

וַיַּרְא אֱלֹהִים אֶת־בְּנֵי
יִשְׂרָאֵל וַיֵּדַע אֱלֹהִים . . .

It is said: "And God saw the people of Israel, and God knew."

All:

וַיַּרְא יי:
זוֹ פְּרִישׁוּת דֶּרֶךְ אֶרֶץ.

God saw: *the enforced separation of husbands and wives.*

Leader:

וַיְצַו פַּרְעֹה לְכָל־עַמּוֹ לֵאמֹר:
כָּל־הַבֵּן הַיִּלּוֹד הַיְאֹרָה
תַּשְׁלִיכֻהוּ.

It is said: "Every son that is born, you shall throw into the Nile."

All:

וַיַּרְא יי: אֵלֶּה הַבָּנִים.

God saw: *the murder of our children.*

Leader:

וְגַם־רָאִיתִי אֶת־הַלַּחַץ
אֲשֶׁר מִצְרַיִם לֹחֲצִים אֹתָם.

And it is said: "Moreover, I have seen how the Egyptians oppress them."

The basic freedom
of the world
is woman's freedom.
A free race
cannot be born
of slave mothers.
A woman enchained
cannot but give
a measure
of that bondage
to her sons
and daughters.
—*Margaret Sanger*

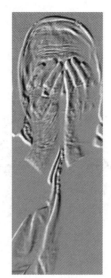

I sit on a man's back, choking him and making him carry me, and yet assure myself and others that I am very sorry for him and wish to lighten his load by all possible means—except by getting off his back. —*Leo Tolstoi*

All:

וַיַּרְא יי: שֶׁגָּזַר פַּרְעֹה לְהַכְנִיעַ וּלְהַשְׁפִּיל רוּחֵנוּ.

God saw: the determination to crush our spirit.

Leader:

וַיַּרְא אֶת־עָנְיֵנוּ.

"And the Eternal saw our plight."

A Reader:

וַיֹּאמֶר יהוה: רָאֹה רָאִיתִי אֶת־עֳנִי עַמִּי אֲשֶׁר בְּמִצְרָיִם, וְאֶת־צַעֲקָתָם שָׁמַעְתִּי מִפְּנֵי נֹגְשָׂיו, כִּי יָדַעְתִּי אֶת־מַכְאֹבָיו.

God said: "How well I see the plight of My people in Egypt; I hear their outcry against their taskmasters. Yes, I know how they suffer."

A Reader:

אֶת־עָנְיֵנוּ וְאֶת־לַחֲצֵנוּ, וְאֶת־עֲמָלֵנוּ.

"Our plight, our woe, our oppression."

Even if you are a slave, forced to labour at some abominable and murderous trade for bread—as iron-forging, for instance, or gunpowder-making—you can resolve to deliver yourself, and your children after you, from the chains of that hell, and from the domination of its slavemasters, or to die… What Egyptian bondage do you suppose… was ever so cruel as a modern English forge, with its steel hammers? What Egyptian worship of garlic or crocodile ever so damnable as modern English worship of money? —*John Ruskin*

Leader:

כְּנֶגֶד הַקָּדוֹשׁ בָּרוּךְ הוּא
דִּבְּרָה הַתּוֹרָה, כַּכָּתוּב:
וַתִּקְצַר נַפְשׁוֹ בַּעֲמַל יִשְׂרָאֵל.
וְעוֹד: בְּכָל־צָרָתָם, לוֹ צָר.

Our plight is God's as well, for
we are taught: "God is diminished
when we are oppressed." And
it is written: "In all their
afflictions, God is afflicted."

A Reader:

וְשָׁנִינוּ:
בְּכָל־מָקוֹם שֶׁגָּלוּ,
שְׁכִינָה עִמָּהֶן.
גָּלוּ לְמִצְרַיִם,
שְׁכִינָה עִמָּהֶן;
גָּלוּ לְבָבֶל, שְׁכִינָה עִמָּהֶן;
וְאַף כְּשֶׁהֵן עֲתִידִין לְהִגָּאֵל,
שְׁכִינָה עִמָּהֶן.

And we have learned:
Whenever we go into exile,
the Divine Presence goes with us.
When we were exiled to Egypt,
the Divine Presence went with us;
in Babylon the Presence was
    with us;
and until the final redemption,
God will remain in exile with us.

The less fit a man
is for the possession of
power—the less likely to
be allowed to exercise it
over any person with that
person's voluntary
consent—the more does
he hug himself in the
consciousness of the
power the law gives him,
exact its legal rights to
the utmost point which
custom (the custom of
men like himself) will
tolerate, and take pleasure
in using the power,
merely to enliven the
agreeable sense of
possessing it.
                —*John Stuart Mill*

A Reader:

וַיּוֹצִאֵנוּ יהוה מִמִּצְרַיִם
בְּיָד חֲזָקָה וּבִזְרֹעַ נְטוּיָה.

"Then God led us out of Egypt with a mighty hand, with an outstretched arm."

All:

לֹא עַל יְדֵי מַלְאָךְ.
וְלֹא עַל יְדֵי שָׂרָף.
וְלֹא עַל יְדֵי שָׁלִיחַ.
אֶלָּא הַקָּדוֹשׁ בָּרוּךְ הוּא
בִּכְבוֹדוֹ וּבְעַצְמוֹ!

Not by an angel.
Not by a seraph.
Not by a messenger.
You Yourself,
the Holy One,
in all Your glory!

Men their rights and nothing more; women their rights and nothing less.
—*Susan B. Anthony and Elizabeth Cady Stanton*

Leader:

וּבְמֹרָא גָּדוֹל וּבְאֹתוֹת
וּבְמֹפְתִים.

"With awesome power, with signs and wonders."

A Reader:

זוֹ גִּלּוּי שְׁכִינָה: כְּמוֹ שֶׁנֶּאֱמַר: אוֹ הֲנִסָּה אֱלֹהִים לָבוֹא
לָקַחַת לוֹ גוֹי מִקֶּרֶב גּוֹי בְּמַסֹּת, בְּאֹתֹת, וּבְמוֹפְתִים,
וּבְמִלְחָמָה, וּבְיָד חֲזָקָה, וּבִזְרוֹעַ נְטוּיָה, וּבְמוֹרָאִים גְּדֹלִים,
כְּכֹל אֲשֶׁר־עָשָׂה לָכֶם יהוה אֱלֹהֵיכֶם בְּמִצְרַיִם לְעֵינֶיךָ?

The Divine Presence reveals itself as liberation. As it is said: "Has any 'god' ever attempted to go and take a nation from the very midst of another nation with awesome power, with signs and wonders, as your God did for you in Egypt before your very eyes?"

Continue on page 41

An Alternative Answer To Our Questions

Leader:

It is written:

All:

*Our ancestors were wandering
Arameans.
They went down to Egypt.
They lived there as strangers,
few in number.
There they became a great nation,
mighty and numerous.
But the Egyptians were cruel to us.*

*They afflicted us.
They imposed hard labor upon us.
Then we cried out to the Eternal
One,
the God of our ancestors.
And the Eternal heard our cry,
saw our plight, our woe,
our oppression.*

Leader:

NOW LET US CALL IT TO MIND:

Our people began as nomads:
As free men and women they came to the land of Canaan.
And though their descendants journeyed to Egypt as welcome guests,
in the end they were enslaved.

All:

*Then God led us out of Egypt
with a mighty hand,
with an outstretched arm,
with awesome power,
with signs and wonders.*

A Reader:

WE REMEMBER the wilderness, our way to the Land of Promise,

A Reader:

the land where the words of prophets and poets became Torah.

A Reader:

They taught: love truth and peace.

A Reader:

A far-off dream, this, for Judah and Jerusalem fell. Solomon's Temple vanished; the people were carried off.

All:

By the rivers of Babylon, there we sat down and wept, as we remembered Zion. On the willows there we hung up our harps. For there our captors demanded of us song, and our tormentors, mirth, saying: "Sing us one of the songs of Zion!" (Psalm 137:1-3)

Leader:

Yet we were delivered from exile, and we began to rebuild.

All:

Break into songs of praise,
O ruins of Jerusalem;
the Eternal will comfort our people,
and set Jerusalem free. (Isaiah 52:9)

Leader:

When Greek invaders oppressed us, we rose up under the banner of the Maccabees.

All:

So it happened that on the very day when the sanctuary had been profaned the cleansing of the Temple took place—on the twenty-fifth day of Kislev.… And they decreed and confirmed by vote that the entire people of the Jews should celebrate these days every year.
(From II Maccabees 10)

Leader:

When Roman power ruled our land, the Pharisees and Rabbis molded a new Torah for a new day.

A Reader:

Jerusalem and the Second Temple became a field of stone, but our people endured, and our spirit was strong: the Spoken Torah began to grow.

All:

Once, as Rabban Yochanan ben Zakkai was coming forth from Jerusalem, Rabbi Joshua, following him, beheld the Temple in ruins. "Woe is us," he lamented, "that the place where Israel found atonement for its sins is laid waste." "Do not grieve, my son," said Yochanan. "We have a means of atonement equally good—deeds of loving kindness, as it is said (Hosea 6:6), It is steadfast love I want, and not sacrifice."

Leader:

This Torah spelled out a faith by which we could live a daily life in holiness.

All:

"My word is like fire ... and like a hammer shattering rock." (Jeremiah 23:29) The School of Rabbi Ishmael interpreted this: "As this hammer creates innumerable sparks, so does a single text yield many meanings." Thus understood, the Torah remained a Tree of Life for our people. (Tanchuma, Noah, §3; Sanhedrin 34a)

Leader:

We went forth to the west and the east, to the north and the south. Some to Jerusalem; others dwelt in the lands of the Arabs, or in Christian Europe: Ashkenaz and Sepharad.

A Reader:

We longed to return to Zion, we prayed for an end to the pain of exile, we endured in hope.

All:

O Zion, will you not ask after your captives—
Those who seek your good, the remnant of your flocks?
From west and east, north and south, from every side,
Accept the blessing of those near and far,
and the blessing of this captive of desire
Who sheds his tears like Hermon's dew
And longs to have them fall upon your hills. (Judah Halevi)

Leader:

The long nightmare of Europe began with the Crusades. WE REMEMBER the expulsion of the Jews of Iberia, the false accusations, massacres, expulsions from lands we had settled long before, ghettos, endless humiliations. Through all this we struggled to remain faithful to our God and our people.

All:

I thought: how can I ask to be free,
When You are imprisoned with me? (Ephraim of Regensburg)

Leader:

NOW WE CALL IT TO MIND: Europe, emerging from Medieval night, found us eager to share in the shaping of a better world. New forms of faith were born, taking root especially in lands of freedom.

A Reader:

The dream of a Zion restored began to be real: Jews streamed to Palestine.

All:

I have not sung to you
or praised your name, my land,
for mighty deeds
and war's victories;
my hands have planted seedlings
by Jordan's quiet shore,
my feet have beaten paths
in lonely forests.
How poor, Mother, how very poor
your daughter's gift.
Only:
a shout of joy at the break of light,
a stifled sob for your pain.
(Rachel Bluestein)

Leader:

We came to the Americas, too, in search of a better life. And we flourished in Germany, in France, in Britain.

A Reader:

But new Pharaohs arose in Europe: Hitler and Stalin. They wrought destruction upon Jews and upon others. A death of the body and a death of the soul: this was the twin aim of these tyrants.

All:

Your glory, O Israel, is slain upon your high places!
How are the mighty fallen!
Saul and Jonathan, beloved and lovely!
In life and in death they were not divided;
they were swifter than eagles,
they were stronger than lions.
How are the mighty fallen in the midst of the battle!   (II Samuel 1:19, 23, 25)

Leader:

But we have outlived those tyrants: out of the ashes of the Shoah arose the Jewish State; and after the oppression of Stalin the Jews of Silence were redeemed: free at last to stay or leave, free at last to be Jews among Jews.

A Reader:

Thus have we been delivered not once but many times. No Pharaoh has lived to see the end of the Jewish people, but we have lived to see the end of many Pharaohs!

A Reader:

Yet much remains to be done, for much of the world is unfree and in pain. Tyranny and injustice continue to be the lot of millions. The eternal lesson of Passover remains: until all are free, none are truly free.

All:

How beautiful upon the mountains are the feet of the herald,
the one who proclaims peace,
who brings tidings of good and proclaims deliverance,
who says to Zion: "Your God reigns."
O ruins of Jerusalem, hear your sentries raise their voices
and shout together in triumph;
for with their own eyes they shall see
the return of the Eternal One to Zion.
And all the world shall see the salvation of our God. (Isaiah 52:7-8, 10)

Leader:

No liberation is easy. As tyranny brings death and terror to its victims, so the struggle to overthrow it claims its casualties. There is no redemption without pain.

Israel suffered greatly before it was redeemed from Egyptian bondage. And we remember that our oppressors suffered many plagues before they were willing to let our people go.

Our rejoicing at the liberation of our ancestors should be tempered by the memory of this suffering of the oppressor and the oppressed, and by the knowledge that tyranny and cruelty still abide: tyrants fall but others rise to take their place. Many evils remain to plague us. Each one diminishes our cup of joy.

All:

A pathy in the face of evil
B rutal torture of the helpless
C ruel mockery of the old and the weak
D espair of human goodness
E nvy of the joy of others
F alsehood and deception corroding our faith
G reedy theft of earth's resources
H atred of learning and culture
I nstigation of war and aggression
J ustice delayed, justice denied, justice mocked....

Leader:

We look back now upon the ancient plagues, the plagues of legend, the signs and wonders that haunt us still:

**A drop of wine is removed from the cup
at the mention of each plague**

עשר מכות | The Ten Plagues

All:

BLOOD	דָּם	*Dam*
FROGS	צְפַרְדֵּעַ	*Ts'far-dei-a*
LICE	כִּנִּים	*Ki-nim*
FLIES	עָרוֹב	*A-rov*
CATTLE DISEASE	דֶּבֶר	*Deh-ver*
BOILS	שְׁחִין	*Sh'chin*
HAIL	בָּרָד	*Ba-rad*
LOCUSTS	אַרְבֶּה	*Ar-beh*
DARKNESS	חֹשֶׁךְ	*Cho-shech*
DEATH OF THE FIRSTBORN	מַכַּת בְּכוֹרוֹת	*Ma-kat B'cho-rot*

Leader:

When the cup of suffering had run over, Egypt's grip was loosened. On that day, Israel went forth to freedom. They made their way to the Sea of Reeds. Cloud by day, fire by night: God's Presence went before them. Pharaoh's heart changed yet again, and he dispatched his troops to recapture the fleeing slaves—for the oppressors' fury grows as their grip begins to weaken, and in their rage they pursue their victims even to their own destruction. Israel stood uncertain: before them the sea, behind them Egypt's host.

A Reader:

כְּשֶׁעָמְדוּ יִשְׂרָאֵל עַל הַיָּם, הָיָה זֶה אוֹמֵר: אֵין אֲנִי יוֹרֵד תְּחִלָּה לַיָּם, וְזֶה אוֹמֵר: אֵין אֲנִי יוֹרֵד תְּחִלָּה לַיָּם. מִתּוֹךְ שֶׁהָיוּ עוֹמְדִין וְנוֹטְלִין עֵצָה אֵלּוּ וָאֵלּוּ, קָפַץ נַחְשׁוֹן בֶּן עַמִּינָדָב וְיָרַד לַיָּם תְּחִלָּה.

AT THAT TIME, when Israel stood at the edge of the sea, each one said, "I will not be the first to enter." While they stood there, Nachshon ben Amminadav leaped into the sea. Only then did the others follow.

A Reader:

בְּשָׁעָה שֶׁיָּרְדוּ יִשְׂרָאֵל לַיָּם, בָּאוּ מַיִם עַד נֶפֶשׁ. מִכָּאן אַתָּה
לָמֵד שֶׁלֹּא נִקְרַע לָהֶם הַיָּם עַד שֶׁבָּאוּ לְתוֹכוֹ עַד חָטְמָן,
וְאַחַר־כָּךְ נַעֲשָׂה לָהֶם יַבָּשָׁה.

AT THAT TIME, they plunged into the waters, going farther
and farther, until it seemed the waters must cover their heads.
Only when they had gone as far as they could through their own
efforts, did the waters part for them!

A Reader:

The people overcame their fear, as all must in every generation
who would be free. For the human fate has been exile and oppression,
again and again; and the human task: to find hope, to overcome.
As it is said:

All:

אַל־תִּירָא, כִּי גְאַלְתִּיךָ; קָרָאתִי בְשִׁמְךָ, לִי־אָתָּה.
כִּי־תַעֲבֹר בַּמַּיִם אִתְּךָ־אָנִי; וּבַנְּהָרוֹת, לֹא יִשְׁטְפוּךָ.

"Have no fear, for I am redeeming you; I have called you by name,
you are Mine. When you pass through the waters, I am with you; when
you pass through the torrents, they shall not overwhelm you."

Leader:

וַיַּרְא יִשְׂרָאֵל אֶת־הַיָּד הַגְּדֹלָה אֲשֶׁר עָשָׂה יהוה בְּמִצְרַיִם,
וַיִּירְאוּ הָעָם אֶת־יהוה . . .
בְּאוֹתָהּ שָׁעָה בִּקְשׁוּ מַלְאֲכֵי הַשָּׁרֵת לוֹמַר שִׁירָה לִפְנֵי
הַקָּדוֹשׁ בָּרוּךְ הוּא. אָמַר לָהֶם הַקָּדוֹשׁ בָּרוּךְ הוּא:
מַעֲשֵׂי יָדַי טוֹבְעִין בַּיָּם, וְאַתֶּם אוֹמְרִים שִׁירָה לְפָנַי!

It is said (Exodus 14): When Israel saw the great deed the Eternal
had done against the Egyptians, the people stood in awe of God.

AT THAT TIME, the ministering angels began to sing a song of
praise before the Holy One; but God rebuked them, saying, "My
children are drowning, and you sing praises!"

All:

O God, teach us to rejoice in freedom, but not in our pursuer's pain.
Let the day come when hate is no more,
and we are free to rejoice without sadness,
to sing without tears.

Leader:

That day is not yet. Since the Exodus we have known many oppressions and deliverances. Often we have suffered, often triumphed and always, as a people, survived. For the Redeemer of Israel has been our never-failing strength. As it is said:

A Reader:

אַל־תִּירָא, כִּי עִמְּךָ־אָנִי; אַל־תִּשְׁתָּע, כִּי־אֲנִי אֱלֹהֶיךָ.
אִמַּצְתִּיךָ, אַף־עֲזַרְתִּיךָ; אַף־תְּמַכְתִּיךָ בִּימִין צִדְקִי.

"Fear not, for I am with you;
do not despair, for I am your God.
I will strengthen you;
1 will help you;
1 will uphold you
with the power of My hand!"

Whoever battles with monsters had better see to it that it does not turn him into a monster. And if you gaze long into an abyss, the abyss will gaze back into you.
—*Friedrich Nietzsche*

The cups are raised

All:

בָּרוּךְ שׁוֹמֵר הַבְטָחָתוֹ לְיִשְׂרָאֵל; בָּרוּךְ הוּא.
וְהִיא שֶׁעָמְדָה לַאֲבוֹתֵינוּ וְלָנוּ;
שֶׁלֹּא אֶחָד בִּלְבַד עָמַד עָלֵינוּ לְכַלּוֹתֵינוּ:
אֶלָּא שֶׁבְּכָל־דּוֹר וָדוֹר עוֹמְדִים עָלֵינוּ לְכַלּוֹתֵינוּ,
וְהַקָּדוֹשׁ בָּרוּךְ הוּא מַצִּילֵינוּ מִיָּדָם.

If you put a chain around the neck of a slave, the other end fastens itself around your own.
—Ralph Waldo Emerson

Blessed is the One who keeps faith with Israel; blessed is our God.
This promise sustained our ancestors; this promise sustains us.
For not only one enemy has sought to destroy us:
in every generation there are those who seek to destroy us,
but the Holy One saves us from their hands.

The cups are set down

Leader:

בְּכָל־דּוֹר וָדוֹר חַיָּב אָדָם לִרְאוֹת אֶת־עַצְמוֹ כְּאִלּוּ הוּא יָצָא
מִמִּצְרָיִם, שֶׁנֶּאֱמַר: וְהִגַּדְתָּ לְבִנְךָ בַּיּוֹם הַהוּא לֵאמֹר, בַּעֲבוּר
זֶה עָשָׂה יהוה לִי בְּצֵאתִי מִמִּצְרָיִם.

In each generation, every one of us must feel that he, that she, has personally gone out of Egypt. As it is said: "You shall tell your child on that day, 'I do this because of what God did for me when I came out of Egypt.'"

All:

לֹא אֶת־אֲבוֹתֵינוּ וְאִמּוֹתֵינוּ בִּלְבַד גָּאַל הַקָּדוֹשׁ בָּרוּךְ הוּא,
אֶלָּא אַף אוֹתָנוּ גָּאַל עִמָּהֶם, שֶׁנֶּאֱמַר: וְאוֹתָנוּ הוֹצִיא מִשָּׁם,
לְמַעַן הָבִיא אֹתָנוּ לָתֶת לָנוּ אֶת־הָאָרֶץ אֲשֶׁר נִשְׁבַּע
לַאֲבֹתֵינוּ.

For the Holy One redeemed not only our ancestors, but us along with them. As it is said: "You led us out of there, that you might bring us to the land You promised to our ancestors."

דַּיֵּנוּ | Dayyénu

♪

p. 96

כַּמָּה מַעֲלוֹת טוֹבוֹת
לַמָּקוֹם עָלֵינוּ!

How many gifts has God
bestowed on us!

אִלּוּ הוֹצִיאָנוּ מִמִּצְרַיִם
וְלֹא סִפֵּק צָרְכֵּנוּ בַּמִּדְבָּר—
דַּיֵּנוּ!

I-lu ho-tzi-a-nu mi-mitz-ra-yim
v'lo si-peik tzor-kei-nu ba-mid-bar
— dayyénu!

אִלּוּ סִפֵּק צָרְכֵּנוּ בַּמִּדְבָּר
וְלֹא נָתַן לָנוּ אֶת־הַשַּׁבָּת—
דַּיֵּנוּ!

I-lu si-peik tzor-kei-nu ba-mid-bar
v'lo na-tan la-nu et ha-shabbat
— dayyénu!

אִלּוּ נָתַן לָנוּ אֶת־הַשַּׁבָּת
וְלֹא נָתַן לָנוּ אֶת־הַתּוֹרָה—
דַּיֵּנוּ!

I-lu na-tan la-nu et ha-shabbat
v'lo na-tan la-nu et ha-torah
— dayyénu!

אִלּוּ נָתַן לָנוּ אֶת־הַתּוֹרָה
וְלֹא הִכְנִיסָנוּ לְאֶרֶץ יִשְׂרָאֵל—
דַּיֵּנוּ!

I-lu na-tan la-nu et ha-torah v'lo
hich-ni-sa-nu l'e-retz Yisrael
— dayyénu!

אִלּוּ הִכְנִיסָנוּ לְאֶרֶץ יִשְׂרָאֵל
וְלֹא שָׁלַח לָנוּ אֶת־הַנְּבִיאִים—
דַּיֵּנוּ!

I-lu hich-ni-sa-nu l'e-retz Yisrael
v'lo sha-lach la-nu et ha-n'vi-im
— dayyénu!

אִלּוּ שָׁלַח לָנוּ אֶת־הַנְּבִיאִים
וְלֹא נְתָנֶנוּ לְאוֹר גּוֹיִים—
דַּיֵּנוּ!

I-lu sha-lach la-nu et ha-n'vi-im
v'lo n'ta-na-nu l'or go-yim
— dayyénu!

אִלּוּ נְתָנֶנוּ לְאוֹר גּוֹיִים
וְלֹא הֶחֱיָנוּ בְּכָל־אַרְצוֹת
תְּפוּצָתֵנוּ—דַּיֵּנוּ!

I-lu n'ta-na-nu l'or go-yim v'lo
he-che-ya-nu b'chol ar-tzot
t'fu-tza-tei-nu— dayyénu!

אִלּוּ הֶחֱיָנוּ בְּכָל־אַרְצוֹת
תְּפוּצָתֵנוּ וְלֹא הֱשִׁיבָנוּ לְאֶרֶץ
אֲבוֹתֵינוּ—דַּיֵּנוּ!

I-lu he-che-ya-nu b'chol ar-tzot
t'fu-tza-tei-nu v'lo he-shi-va-nu
l'e-retz a-vo-tei-nu— dayyénu!

אִלּוּ הֱשִׁיבָנוּ לְאֶרֶץ אִמּוֹתֵינוּ
וְלֹא צִוְּנוּ לְתַקֵּן עוֹלָמוֹ—דַּיֵּנוּ!

I-lu he-shi-va-nu l'e-retz
i-mo-tei-nu v'lo tzi-va-nu
l'ta-kein o-la-mo— dayyénu!

Had we been brought out of Egypt and not been supported
in the wilderness
—It would have been enough!

Had we been supported in the wilderness and not been
given the Sabbath
—It would have been enough!

Had we been given the Sabbath and not been given the Torah
—It would have been enough!

Had we been given the Torah and not been brought to
the land of Israel
—It would have been enough!

Had we been brought to the land of Israel and not been
sent the prophets
—It would have been enough!

Had we been sent the prophets and not been called to
be a light to the nations
—It would have been enough!

Had we been called to be a light to the nations and not been
sustained wherever we have dwelt
—It would have been enough!

Had we been sustained wherever we have dwelt and not been
returned to the land of our ancestors
—It would have been enough!

Had we been returned to the land of our ancestors and not
been summoned to perfect this world
—It would have been enough!

IF WE were delivered from bondage while others remained enslaved,
could we say "Dayyenu?"

IF WE could be at peace while others died in wars,
could we say "Dayyenu?"

IF WE were born to prosper while others were born to weep,
could we say "Dayyenu?"

IF WE alone were chosen while others were forgotten,
could we say "Dayyenu?"

AND IF WE have enough to eat while others starve,
can we say "Dayyenu?"

AND IF OUR houses are safe while others live in fear,
can we say "Dayyenu?"

AND IF WE have a land to live on while others are far from home,
can we say "Dayyenu?" (CS)

What constitutes the bulwark of our own liberty and independence? It is not our frowning battlements, our bristling sea coasts, our army and our navy. These are not our reliance against tyranny. All of these may be turned against us without making us weaker for the struggle. Our reliance is the love of liberty which God has planted in us. Our defense is in the spirit which prizes liberty as the heritage of all men, in all lands everywhere. Destroy this spirit and you have planted the seeds of despotism at your own doors. Familiarize yourselves with the chains of bondage and you prepare your own limbs to wear them. —*Abraham Lincoln*

Leader:

עַל אַחַת כַּמָּה וְכַמָּה
טוֹבָה כְפוּלָה וּמְכֻפֶּלֶת
לַמָּקוֹם עָלֵינוּ!

How much more then, O God,
must we thank You for Your
boundless goodness to us!

All:

שֶׁהוֹצִיאָנוּ מִמִּצְרַיִם,
וְסִפֵּק צָרְכֵּנוּ בַּמִּדְבָּר,
וְנָתַן לָנוּ אֶת־הַשַּׁבָּת,
וְנָתַן לָנוּ אֶת־הַתּוֹרָה,
וְהִכְנִיסָנוּ לְאֶרֶץ יִשְׂרָאֵל,
וְשָׁלַח לָנוּ אֶת־הַנְּבִיאִים,
וּנְתָנֶנוּ לְאוֹר גּוֹיִים,
וְהֶחֱיָנוּ בְּכָל־אַרְצוֹת
תְּפוּצָתֵנוּ,
וֶהֱשִׁיבָנוּ לְאֶרֶץ אֲבוֹתֵינוּ
וְאִמּוֹתֵינוּ, וְצִוָּנוּ
לְתַקֵּן עוֹלָם בְּמַלְכוּת שַׁדַּי!

For You brought us out of Egypt,
supported us in the wilderness,
gave us the Sabbath,
gave us the Torah,
brought us to the land of Israel,
sent us the prophets,
called us to be a light to the
    nations,
sustained us wherever we have
    dwelt,
returned us to the land of our
    ancestors,
and summoned us to perfect this
    world under Your unchallenged
    rule!

The cups are raised

Leader:

לְפִיכָךְ אֲנַחְנוּ חַיָּבִים לְהוֹדוֹת, לְהַלֵּל, לְשַׁבֵּחַ, לְפָאֵר,
לְרוֹמֵם, לְהַדֵּר, לְבָרֵךְ, לְעַלֵּה, וּלְקַלֵּס לְמִי שֶׁעָשָׂה
לַאֲבוֹתֵינוּ וּלְאִמּוֹתֵינוּ וְלָנוּ אֶת־כָּל־הַנִּסִּים הָאֵלּוּ.

Therefore we thank, bless, and praise beyond measure the One
who performed all these wonders for our ancestors and for us;

Whoever walked behind anyone to freedom? If we can't go hand in hand, I don't want to go. —Hazel Scott

To move freely you must be deeply rooted. —Bella Lewitzky

All:

שֶׁהוֹצִיאָנוּ   *who led us*

מֵעַבְדוּת לְחֵרוּת,   *from bondage to freedom,*

מִיָּגוֹן לְשִׂמְחָה,   *from anguish to joy,*

מֵאֵבֶל לְיוֹם טוֹב,   *from mourning to celebration,*

וּמֵאֲפֵלָה לְאוֹר גָּדוֹל,   *from darkness to light,*

וּמִשִּׁעְבּוּד לִגְאֻלָּה.   *from subjection to redemption.*

Leader:

וְנֹאמַר לְפָנָיו   Let us then sing before God

שִׁירָה חֲדָשָׁה הַלְלוּיָהּ.   a song ever new! Halleluyah!

"The dove came back to him toward evening, and there in her bill was a plucked-off olive leaf!" (Genesis 8:11)

Where did she get it? Rabbi Bebai said: The gates of the Garden of Eden opened; she brought it out of there. Rabbi Aibo said: If she were coming from the Garden of Eden, she would have brought something more exotic, like cinnamon or balsam. But the point of the story is not where she came from but what she brought: the olive leaf was a sign to Noah, saying: "Noah, better this bitter thing from the hand of the Holy One, than a sweet thing from your hand." (Midrash)

It is by the goodness of God that in our country we have those three unspeakably precious things: freedom of speech, freedom of conscience, and the prudence never to practice either of them.

—*Mark Twain*

Whatever the human law may be, neither an individual nor a nation can ever deliberately commit the least act of injustice without having to pay the penalty for it.

—*Henry David Thoreau*

הלל חלק ראשון | Hallel, First Part

Psalm 113

הַלְלוּיָהּ! הַלְלוּ עַבְדֵי יהוה, הַלְלוּ אֶת־שֵׁם יהוה.

יְהִי שֵׁם יהוה מְבֹרָךְ מֵעַתָּה וְעַד־עוֹלָם.

מִמִּזְרַח־שֶׁמֶשׁ עַד־מְבוֹאוֹ מְהֻלָּל שֵׁם יהוה.

רָם עַל־כָּל־גּוֹיִם יהוה, עַל הַשָּׁמַיִם כְּבוֹדוֹ.

מִי כַּיהוה אֱלֹהֵינוּ, הַמַּגְבִּיהִי לָשָׁבֶת,

הַמַּשְׁפִּילִי לִרְאוֹת בַּשָּׁמַיִם וּבָאָרֶץ?

מְקִימִי מֵעָפָר דָּל, מֵאַשְׁפֹּת יָרִים אֶבְיוֹן.

לְהוֹשִׁיבִי עִם־נְדִיבִים, עִם נְדִיבֵי עַמּוֹ.

מוֹשִׁיבִי עֲקֶרֶת הַבַּיִת, אֵם־הַבָּנִים שְׂמֵחָה, הַלְלוּיָהּ!

Halleluyah!
Sing praises, you servants of the Eternal One,
praise the name of God.
> *Blessed is the name of God,*
> *now and forever.*
From sunrise to sunset, praised be the name of God.
> *The Eternal is supreme above the nations;*
> *God's glory is higher than the heavens.*
Who is like the Eternal our God
in heaven and on earth?
> *Who so exalted, and yet so near:*
Who raises the poor from the dust,
> *who lifts the wretched from the dung,*
Giving them a place among rulers,
> *among the leaders of the people,*
Making all who are barren,
> *the joyful parents of children. Halleluyah!*

p. 97

Psalm 114

בְּצֵאת יִשְׂרָאֵל מִמִּצְרָיִם, בֵּית יַעֲקֹב מֵעַם לֹעֵז,
הָיְתָה יְהוּדָה לְקָדְשׁוֹ, יִשְׂרָאֵל מַמְשְׁלוֹתָיו.
הַיָּם רָאָה וַיָּנֹס, הַיַּרְדֵּן יִסֹּב לְאָחוֹר.
הֶהָרִים רָקְדוּ כְאֵילִים, גְּבָעוֹת כִּבְנֵי־צֹאן.
מַה־לְּךָ הַיָּם כִּי תָנוּס, הַיַּרְדֵּן תִּסֹּב לְאָחוֹר?
הֶהָרִים תִּרְקְדוּ כְאֵילִים, גְּבָעוֹת כִּבְנֵי־צֹאן?
מִלִּפְנֵי אָדוֹן חוּלִי אָרֶץ, מִלִּפְנֵי אֱלוֹהַּ יַעֲקֹב.
הַהֹפְכִי הַצּוּר אֲגַם־מָיִם, חַלָּמִישׁ לְמַעְיְנוֹ־מָיִם.

When Israel went forth from Egypt,
the House of Jacob from an alien people,
 Judah became God's sanctuary,
 Israel, God's dominion.
The sea saw it and fled,
 the Jordan turned back.
The mountains skipped like rams,
 the hills like young lambs.
What ails you, O sea, that you run away?
 O Jordan, that you turn back?
O mountains, why do you skip like rams?
 Why, O hills, like young lambs?
Dance, O earth, before the Eternal;
before the God of Israel,
 Who turns the rock into a pool of water,
 the stony ground into a flowing spring.

כוס שני | The Second Cup

I will deliver you. For the escape from servitude is not yet freedom. The slave has to free him/her-self from more than physical bonds. There remain pain, anger, the habits of serfdom, the sense of worthlessness instilled in us by our conditioning. For all this, comes the second promise: I will deliver you.

Leader:

We raise our cups in remembrance of the second promise of redemption, as it is said:

All:

וְהִצַּלְתִּי אֶתְכֶם מֵעֲבֹדָתָם.

V'HI-TZAL-TI et-chem mei-a-vo-da-tam.
I will DELIVER YOU from their bondage.

A Reader:

בָּרוּךְ אַתָּה יי אֱלֹהֵינוּ מֶלֶךְ הָעוֹלָם, אֲשֶׁר גְּאָלָנוּ וְגָאַל
אֶת־אֲבוֹתֵינוּ וְאִמּוֹתֵינוּ מִמִּצְרַיִם, וְהִגִּיעָנוּ לַלַּיְלָה הַזֶּה
לֶאֱכָל־בּוֹ מַצָּה וּמָרוֹר. כֵּן, יי אֱלֹהֵינוּ וֵאלֹהֵי אֲבוֹתֵינוּ
וְאִמּוֹתֵינוּ, הַגִּיעֵנוּ לְמוֹעֲדִים וְלִרְגָלִים אֲחֵרִים הַבָּאִים
לִקְרָאתֵנוּ לְשָׁלוֹם, שְׂמֵחִים בְּבִנְיַן עִירֶךָ וְשָׂשִׂים בַּעֲבוֹדָתֶךָ.
וְנוֹדֶה־לְּךָ שִׁיר חָדָשׁ עַל גְּאֻלָּתֵנוּ, וְעַל פְּדוּת נַפְשֵׁנוּ.
בָּרוּךְ אַתָּה יי גָּאַל יִשְׂרָאֵל.

We praise You, Eternal One. You have redeemed us and our ancestors from Egypt and enabled us to celebrate our freedom this night with Matzah and Maror. Our God and God of all generations, be with us on all our holy and festive days; may they find us living in peace, building Your City in gladness, and serving You in joy. Then shall we sing to You a new song of thanks, for the deliverance of the world from oppression and the redemption of the spirit from darkness. We praise You, Eternal God, Redeemer of Israel.

All:

בָּרוּךְ אַתָּה יי אֱלֹהֵינוּ מֶלֶךְ
הָעוֹלָם, בּוֹרֵא פְּרִי הַגָּפֶן.

Ba-ruch a-ta Adonai, Eh-lo-hei-nu me-lech ha-o-lam, bo-rei p'ri ha-ga-fen.

We praise You, Eternal One, for the fruit of the vine.

All now drink the second cup

p. 94

הסעודה | The Meal

שלחן עורך

The Meal Is Served

צפון *Tzafun*

At the conclusion of the meal the Afikoman is eaten. Thus, as promised earlier, the lost is found, the hidden revealed, the broken made whole. The children seek and find the Afikoman toward the end of the meal, or the leader seeks and fails to find it. In either case, it is eventually "found" by the children, who receive a reward for their efforts. The meal ends with the eating of the Matzah of the Afikoman.

Before the Afikoman is eaten this might be said:

This Matzah is called צָפוּן *tzafun*, that which was "hidden or stored up." So we pray to the God of our ancestors and God of our descendants: May the time come when the lost will be found, the broken made whole, the hidden revealed. As it is said:

מָה רַב־טוּבְךָ אֲשֶׁר־צָפַנְתָּ לִירֵאֶיךָ!

How great is the goodness You have stored up for those who revere You! *(Psalm 31:20)*

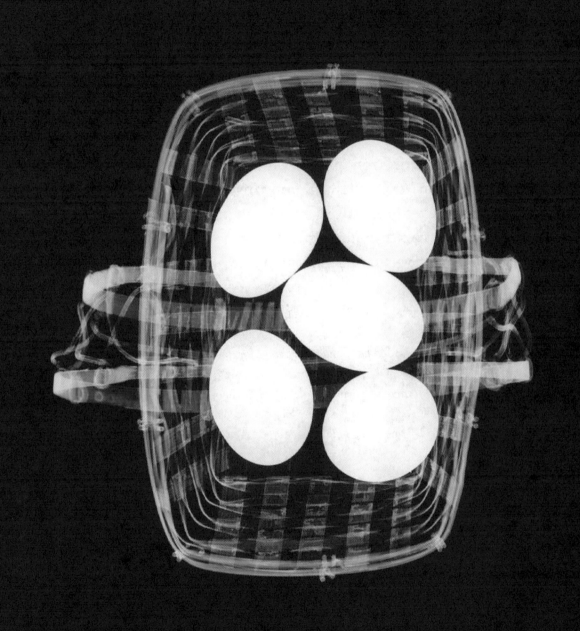

ברך | Thanksgiving for the Meal
The cups are refilled

For a short form of Thanksgiving read the shaded passages.

Psalm 126

All:

A PILGRIM SONG שִׁיר הַמַּעֲלוֹת

בְּשׁוּב יהוה אֶת־שִׁיבַת צִיּוֹן, הָיִינוּ כְּחֹלְמִים. אָז יִמָּלֵא שְׂחוֹק
פִּינוּ, וּלְשׁוֹנֵנוּ רִנָּה. אָז יֹאמְרוּ בַגּוֹיִם: הִגְדִּיל יהוה לַעֲשׂוֹת
עִם־אֵלֶּה. הִגְדִּיל יהוה לַעֲשׂוֹת עִמָּנוּ, הָיִינוּ שְׂמֵחִים!
שׁוּבָה יהוה אֶת־שְׁבִיתֵנוּ, כַּאֲפִיקִים בַּנֶּגֶב. הַזֹּרְעִים בְּדִמְעָה
בְּרִנָּה יִקְצֹרוּ. הָלוֹךְ יֵלֵךְ וּבָכֹה, נֹשֵׂא מֶשֶׁךְ־הַזָּרַע, בֹּא־יָבוֹא
בְרִנָּה, נֹשֵׂא אֲלֻמֹּתָיו.

When God restores the exiles to Zion, it will seem like a dream.
Our mouths will fill with laughter, our tongues with joyful song. They
will say among the nations: God has done great things for them. Yes,
God is doing great things for us, and we are joyful. Restore our
fortunes, O God, as streams revive the desert. Then those who
have sown in tears shall reap in joy. Those who go forth weeping, car-
rying bags of seeds, shall come home with shouts of joy, bearing their
sheaves.

חֲבֵרִים וַחֲבֵרוֹת, נְבָרֵךְ.
יְהִי שֵׁם יי מְבֹרָךְ מֵעַתָּה וְעַד עוֹלָם.

Let us praise God.

Praised be the name of God, now and forever!

בִּרְשׁוּת הַחֶבְרָה, נְבָרֵךְ אֱלֹהֵינוּ שֶׁאָכַלְנוּ מִשֶּׁלּוֹ.
בָּרוּךְ אֱלֹהֵינוּ שֶׁאָכַלְנוּ מִשֶּׁלּוֹ, וּבְטוּבוֹ חָיִינוּ.

Praised be our God, of whose abundance we have eaten.
Praised be our God, of whose abundance we have eaten,
and by whose goodness we live.

בָּרוּךְ הוּא וּבָרוּךְ שְׁמוֹ!

Praised be the Eternal God!

בָּרוּךְ אַתָּה יי אֱלֹהֵינוּ מֶלֶךְ הָעוֹלָם, הַזָּן אֶת־הָעוֹלָם כֻּלּוֹ
בְּטוּבוֹ, בְּחֵן בְּחֶסֶד וּבְרַחֲמִים. הוּא נוֹתֵן לֶחֶם לְכָל־בָּשָׂר,
כִּי לְעוֹלָם חַסְדּוֹ. וּבְטוּבוֹ הַגָּדוֹל תָּמִיד לֹא חָסַר לָנוּ,
וְאַל יֶחְסַר לָנוּ, מָזוֹן לְעוֹלָם וָעֶד, בַּעֲבוּר שְׁמוֹ הַגָּדוֹל.
כִּי הוּא אֵל זָן וּמְפַרְנֵס לַכֹּל, וּמֵטִיב לַכֹּל וּמֵכִין מָזוֹן
לְכָל־בְּרִיּוֹתָיו אֲשֶׁר בָּרָא. בָּרוּךְ אַתָּה יי הַזָּן אֶת־הַכֹּל.

Sovereign God of the universe, we praise You: Your goodness
sustains the world. You are the God of grace, love, and compassion,
the source of bread for all who live—for Your love is everlasting.
In Your great goodness we need never lack for food; You provide
food enough for all.

We praise You, O God, Source of food for all who live.

נוֹדֶה לְךָ, יי אֱלֹהֵינוּ, עַל שֶׁהִנְחַלְתָּ לַאֲבוֹתֵינוּ וּלְאִמּוֹתֵינוּ
אֶרֶץ חֶמְדָּה טוֹבָה וּרְחָבָה; וְעַל שֶׁהוֹצֵאתָנוּ מֵאֶרֶץ מִצְרַיִם;
וּפְדִיתָנוּ מִבֵּית עֲבָדִים; וְעַל בְּרִיתְךָ שֶׁחָתַמְתָּ בִּלְבָבֵנוּ; וְעַל
תּוֹרָתְךָ שֶׁלִּמַּדְתָּנוּ, וְעַל חֻקֶּיךָ שֶׁהוֹדַעְתָּנוּ, וְעַל חַיִּים חֵן
וָחֶסֶד שֶׁחוֹנַנְתָּנוּ, וְעַל אֲכִילַת מָזוֹן שָׁאַתָּה זָן וּמְפַרְנֵס אוֹתָנוּ
תָּמִיד, בְּכָל־יוֹם וּבְכָל־עֵת וּבְכָל־שָׁעָה.

For this good earth that you have entrusted to our mothers and fathers, and to
us; for our deliverance from bondage; for the covenant You have sealed into our
hearts; for Your life-giving love and grace; for Torah, our way of life, and for the
food that sustains us day by day, we give You thanks.

וְעַל הַכֹּל, יי אֱלֹהֵינוּ, אֲנַחְנוּ מוֹדִים לָךְ וּמְבָרְכִים אוֹתָךְ.
יִתְבָּרַךְ שִׁמְךָ בְּפִי כָּל־חַי תָּמִיד לְעוֹלָם וָעֶד, כַּכָּתוּב:
וְאָכַלְתָּ וְשָׂבָעְתָּ, וּבֵרַכְתָּ אֶת־יהוה אֱלֹהֶיךָ עַל־הָאָרֶץ
הַטּוֹבָה אֲשֶׁר נָתַן־לָךְ. בָּרוּךְ אַתָּה יי עַל־הָאָרֶץ וְעַל־הַמָּזוֹן.

For all this we thank You. Let Your praise ever be on the lips of all who live,
as it is written: "When you have eaten and are satisfied, give praise to your God
who has given you this good earth."

We praise You, O God, for the earth, and for its sustenance. Amen.

רַחֵם, יי אֱלֹהֵינוּ, עַל יִשְׂרָאֵל עַמֶּךָ, וְעַל יְרוּשָׁלַיִם עִירֶךָ,
וְעַל צִיּוֹן מִשְׁכַּן כְּבוֹדֶךָ. אֱלֹהֵינוּ אָבִינוּ, רְעֵנוּ זוּנֵנוּ,
פַּרְנְסֵנוּ וְכַלְכְּלֵנוּ וְהַרְוִיחֵנוּ, וְהַרְוַח לָנוּ, יי אֱלֹהֵינוּ,
מְהֵרָה מִכָּל־צָרוֹתֵינוּ. וְנָא אַל תַּצְרִיכֵנוּ, יי אֱלֹהֵינוּ,
לֹא לִידֵי מַתְּנַת בָּשָׂר וָדָם וְלֹא לִידֵי הַלְוָאָתָם, כִּי אִם
לְיָדְךָ הַמְּלֵאָה, הַפְּתוּחָה, הַגְּדוּשָׁה, וְהָרְחָבָה שֶׁלֹּא נֵבוֹשׁ
וְלֹא נִכָּלֵם לְעוֹלָם וָעֶד.

Eternal God, Source of our being, show compassion for Israel Your people, Jerusalem
Your city, and Zion, the ancient dwelling-place of Your glory. Guide and sustain us in
all our habitations, and be a help to us in all our troubles. May we ever be able to help
ourselves and one another, even as we rely on Your open and generous bounty.

On Shabbat Only:

רְצֵה וְהַחֲלִיצֵנוּ, יי אֱלֹהֵינוּ, בְּמִצְוֹתֶיךָ וּבְמִצְוַת יוֹם הַשְּׁבִיעִי
הַשַּׁבָּת הַגָּדוֹל וְהַקָּדוֹשׁ הַזֶּה, כִּי יוֹם זֶה גָּדוֹל וְקָדוֹשׁ הוּא
לְפָנֶיךָ, לִשְׁבָּת־בּוֹ וְלָנוּחַ בּוֹ בְּאַהֲבָה כְּמִצְוַת רְצוֹנֶךָ.
וּבִרְצוֹנְךָ הָנַח לָנוּ, יי אֱלֹהֵינוּ, שֶׁלֹּא תְהֵא צָרָה וְיָגוֹן וַאֲנָחָה
בְּיוֹם מְנוּחָתֵנוּ. וְהַרְאֵנוּ, יי אֱלֹהֵינוּ, בְּנֶחָמַת צִיּוֹן עִירֶךָ
וּבְבִנְיַן יְרוּשָׁלַיִם עִיר קָדְשֶׁךָ, כִּי אַתָּה הוּא בַּעַל הַיְשׁוּעוֹת
וּבַעַל הַנֶּחָמוֹת.

Eternal God, strengthen our resolve to live by Your Mitzvot,
and especially the Mitzvah of the seventh day, the great and holy
Sabbath, the day of rest and serenity, of loving reflection upon
Your will. Father of deliverance, Mother of consolation, give us
this day rest from sorrow, anguish, and pain, and renew our
vision of a more beautiful world.

אֱלֹהֵינוּ וֵאלֹהֵי אֲבוֹתֵינוּ וְאִמּוֹתֵינוּ, יַעֲלֶה וְיָבֹא וְיִזָּכֵר
זִכְרוֹנֵנוּ וְזִכְרוֹן כָּל־עַמְּךָ בֵּית יִשְׂרָאֵל לְפָנֶיךָ, לְטוֹבָה
וְלִבְרָכָה, לְחַיִּים וּלְשָׁלוֹם, בְּיוֹם חַג הַמַּצּוֹת הַזֶּה.
זָכְרֵנוּ, יי אֱלֹהֵינוּ, בּוֹ לְטוֹבָה. אָמֵן.
וּפָקְדֵנוּ בוֹ לִבְרָכָה. אָמֵן.
וְהוֹשִׁיעֵנוּ בוֹ לְחַיִּים. אָמֵן.

Our God and God of all ages, be mindful of us and of all Your people of the House
of Israel. Grant us well-being and blessing, life and peace, on this Feast of Pesach.
Remember us this day for well-being.
Bless us this day with Your presence.
Help us this day to lead a full life.

וּבְנֵה יְרוּשָׁלַיִם עִיר הַקֹּדֶשׁ בִּמְהֵרָה בְיָמֵינוּ.
בָּרוּךְ אַתָּה יי בּוֹנֵה בְרַחֲמָיו יְרוּשָׁלָיִם. אָמֵן.

Let Jerusalem, the holy city, be renewed in our time.
We praise You, O God: in compassion You rebuild Jerusalem. Amen.

בָּרוּךְ אַתָּה יי אֱלֹהֵינוּ מֶלֶךְ הָעוֹלָם, הָאֵל אָבִינוּ אַמֵּינוּ,
אַדִּירֵנוּ, בּוֹרְאֵנוּ, גּוֹאֲלֵנוּ, יוֹצְרֵנוּ, קְדוֹשֵׁנוּ, קְדוֹשׁ יַעֲקֹב,
רוֹעֵנוּ, רוֹעֵה יִשְׂרָאֵל, הַמֶּלֶךְ הַטּוֹב וְהַמֵּטִיב לַכֹּל,
שֶׁבְּכָל־יוֹם וָיוֹם הוּא הֵטִיב, הוּא מֵטִיב, הוּא יֵטִיב לָנוּ.
הוּא גְמָלָנוּ, הוּא גוֹמְלֵנוּ, הוּא יִגְמְלֵנוּ לָעַד, לְחֵן, לְחֶסֶד,
וּלְרַחֲמִים, וּלְרֶוַח, הַצָּלָה וְהַצְלָחָה, בְּרָכָה וִישׁוּעָה, נֶחָמָה,
פַּרְנָסָה וְכַלְכָּלָה, וְרַחֲמִים וְחַיִּים וְשָׁלוֹם, וְכָל־טוֹב,
וּמִכָּל־טוּב אַל־יְחַסְּרֵנוּ.

We praise You, divine Parent of Israel, Source of liberating power and vision,
of all that is holy and good.

You have shown us love and kindness always; day by day You grant us grace
and compassion, deliverance and freedom, prosperity and blessing, life and peace.

הָרַחֲמָן הוּא יִמְלוֹךְ עָלֵינוּ לְעוֹלָם וָעֶד.

Merciful One, be our God forever.

הָרַחֲמָן הוּא יִתְבָּרַךְ בַּשָּׁמַיִם וּבָאָרֶץ.

Merciful One, heaven and earth alike are blessed by Your presence.

הָרַחֲמָן הוּא יִשְׁתַּבַּח לְדוֹר דּוֹרִים וְיִתְפָּאַר בָּנוּ לָנֶצַח
נְצָחִים וְיִתְהַדַּר בָּנוּ לָעַד וּלְעוֹלְמֵי עוֹלָמִים.

Merciful One, let all the generations proclaim Your glory.

הָרַחֲמָן הוּא יְפַרְנְסֵנוּ בְּכָבוֹד.

Merciful One, help us to sustain ourselves in honor.

הָרַחֲמָן הוּא יִשְׁבּוֹר עֻלֵנוּ מֵעַל צַוָּארֵנוּ.

Merciful One, help us break the yoke of oppression from off our necks.

הָרַחֲמָן הוּא יִשְׁלַח בְּרָכָה מְרֻבָּה בַּבַּיִת הַזֶּה
וְעַל שֻׁלְחָן זֶה שֶׁאָכַלְנוּ עָלָיו.

Merciful One, bless this house, this table at which we have eaten.

הָרַחֲמָן הוּא יִשְׁלַח לָנוּ אֶת־אֵלִיָּהוּ הַנָּבִיא זָכוּר לַטּוֹב
וִיבַשֶּׂר־לָנוּ בְּשׂוֹרוֹת טוֹבוֹת יְשׁוּעוֹת וְנֶחָמוֹת.

*Merciful One, send us Elijah-tidings, glimpses of good to come, of redemption and
consolation.*

הָרַחֲמָן הוּא יְזַכֵּנוּ לִימוֹת הַגְּאוּלָה וּלְחַיֵּי הָעוֹלָם הַבָּא.

*Merciful One, find us worthy of witnessing a time of redemption and of
attaining eternal life.*

One or more of the following may be added here:

הָרַחֲמָן הוּא קֶרֶן לְעַמּוֹ יָרִים.

Merciful One, give strength to Your people.

הָרַחֲמָן הוּא יִשְׁלַח בְּרָכָה וְהַצְלָחָה בְּכָל־מַעֲשֵׂי יָדֵינוּ.

Merciful One, bless and prosper the work of our hands.

הָרַחֲמָן הוּא יִרְפָּאֵנוּ רְפוּאָה שְׁלֵמָה רְפוּאַת הַנֶּפֶשׁ
וּרְפוּאַת הַגּוּף.

Merciful One, grant us health of body and spirit.

הָרַחֲמָן הוּא יִפְרֹשׂ עָלֵינוּ סֻכַּת שְׁלוֹמוֹ.

Merciful One, spread over us the shelter of Your peace.

הָרַחֲמָן הוּא יִטַּע תּוֹרָתוֹ וְאַהֲבָתוֹ בְּלִבֵּנוּ וְיָאִיר עֵינֵינוּ
בִּמְאוֹר תּוֹרָתוֹ.

Merciful One, implant Your teaching and Your love in our hearts and illumine
our eyes with the light of Torah.

הָרַחֲמָן הוּא יְמַלֵּא מִשְׁאֲלוֹת לִבֵּנוּ לְטוֹבָה.

Merciful One, fulfill for good the desires of our hearts.

הָרַחֲמָן, הוּא יְבָרֵךְ אוֹתָנוּ וְאֶת־כָּל־אֲשֶׁר לָנוּ, כְּמוֹ
שֶׁנִּתְבָּרְכוּ אֲבוֹתֵינוּ אַבְרָהָם, יִצְחָק, וְיַעֲקֹב, וְאִמּוֹתֵינוּ
שָׂרָה, רִבְקָה, לֵאָה וְרָחֵל, בַּכֹּל מִכֹּל כֹּל, כֵּן יְבָרֵךְ
אוֹתָנוּ כֻּלָּנוּ יַחַד, בִּבְרָכָה שְׁלֵמָה, וְנֹאמַר: אָמֵן.

*Merciful One, bless us and all our dear ones; as You blessed our
ancestors Abraham, Isaac, and Jacob; Sarah, Rebekah, Leah, and
Rachel, so bless us, one and all; and let us say: Amen.*

בַּמָּרוֹם יְלַמְּדוּ עָלֵינוּ זְכוּת שֶׁתְּהֵא לְמִשְׁמֶרֶת שָׁלוֹם; וְנִשָּׂא
בְרָכָה מֵאֵת יי וּצְדָקָה מֵאֱלֹהֵי יִשְׁעֵנוּ, וְנִמְצָא־חֵן וְשֵׂכֶל
טוֹב בְּעֵינֵי אֱלֹהִים וְאָדָם.

May we receive blessings from the Eternal, kindness from God
our help, and may we all find divine and human grace and favor.

On Shabbat Only:

הָרַחֲמָן, הוּא יַנְחִילֵנוּ יוֹם שֶׁכֻּלּוֹ שַׁבָּת.

Merciful One, help us to see the coming of a time that is all Shabbat.

הָרַחֲמָן, הוּא יַנְחִילֵנוּ יוֹם שֶׁכֻּלּוֹ טוֹב.

Merciful One, help us to see the coming of a time that is all good.

עֹשֶׂה שָׁלוֹם בִּמְרוֹמָיו הוּא
יַעֲשֶׂה שָׁלוֹם עָלֵינוּ
וְעַל־כָּל־יִשְׂרָאֵל,
וְאִמְרוּ אָמֵן.

May the Source of perfect peace grant peace to us, to all Israel, and to all the world.

הֹדוּ לַיהוה כִּי־טוֹב,
כִּי לְעוֹלָם חַסְדּוֹ.
פּוֹתֵחַ אֶת־יָדֶךָ
וּמַשְׂבִּיעַ לְכָל־חַי רָצוֹן.
בָּרוּךְ הַגֶּבֶר אֲשֶׁר יִבְטַח
בַּיהוה, וְהָיָה יהוה מִבְטַחוֹ.
יהוה עֹז לְעַמּוֹ יִתֵּן,
יהוה יְבָרֵךְ אֶת־עַמּוֹ בַשָּׁלוֹם.

Give thanks to God, who is good, whose love is everlasting, *whose hand is open to feed all that lives.*

Blessed are you who trust in God; God is Your stronghold.

Eternal God: give strength to Your people; Eternal God: bless Your people with peace.

כוס של ברכה │ The Third Cup

The third stage of our ascent to freedom brings us beyond
"freedom from…" into the realm of "freedom for…." Now we
begin to see a world of growing possibility, that we can create
for ourselves: I am, therefore I was born to be free, born
in the divine image to be a creator. Delivered from inner
bondage, we are redeemed to be what we can be.
This cup is called the "Cup of Blessing."

Leader:

We raise our cups in remembrance of the third promise of
redemption, as it is said:

All:

וְגָאַלְתִּי אֶתְכֶם בִּזְרוֹעַ נְטוּיָה.

V'GA-AL-TI et-chem biz-ro-a n'tu-yah…
I will REDEEM YOU *with outstretched arm.*

בָּרוּךְ אַתָּה יי אֱלֹהֵינוּ מֶלֶךְ
הָעוֹלָם, בּוֹרֵא פְּרִי הַגָּפֶן.

*Ba-ruch a-ta Adonai, Eh-lo-hei-nu
me-lech ha-o-lam, bo-rei p'ri
ha-ga-fen.*

We praise You, Eternal One, for the fruit of the vine.

All now drink the third cup

The following section may be read wholly or in part.

"The Cup of Elijah" begins on page 68.

הלל חלק שני | Hallel, Second Part

(The omission of Psalms 115 and 116 is explained in the Notes)

Psalm 117

הַלְלוּ אֶת־יהוה, כָּל־גּוֹיִם;
שַׁבְּחוּהוּ, כָּל־הָאֻמִּים,
כִּי גָבַר עָלֵינוּ חַסְדּוֹ;
וֶאֱמֶת־יהוה לְעוֹלָם,
הַלְלוּיָהּ!

Praise God, all you nations; extol the Eternal One, all you peoples, for great is God's love toward us; the Eternal One's faithfulness is everlasting. Halleluyah!

From Psalm 118

הוֹדוּ לַיהוה כִּי־טוֹב כִּי לְעוֹלָם חַסְדּוֹ.
יֹאמַר־נָא יִשְׂרָאֵל: כִּי לְעוֹלָם חַסְדּוֹ.
יֹאמְרוּ־נָא בֵית־אַהֲרֹן: כִּי לְעוֹלָם חַסְדּוֹ.
יֹאמְרוּ־נָא יִרְאֵי יהוה: כִּי לְעוֹלָם חַסְדּוֹ.
מִן־הַמֵּצַר קָרָאתִי יָּהּ, עָנָנִי בַמֶּרְחָב יָהּ.
יהוה לִי, לֹא אִירָא; מַה־יַּעֲשֶׂה לִי אָדָם?
יהוה לִי בְּעֹזְרָי וַאֲנִי אֶרְאֶה בְשֹׂנְאָי.

Give thanks to the Eternal One, who is good,
   whose love is everlasting.

Let Israel declare:
   God's love is everlasting.

Let the House of Aaron declare:
   God's love is everlasting.

Let all the world declare:
   God's love is everlasting.

In my distress I cried out to God,
   who answered me and set me free.

God is with me, I am not afraid;
   what can others do to me?

With God as my helper
   I can face any foe.

טוֹב לַחֲסוֹת בַּיהוה מִבְּטֹחַ בָּאָדָם.

טוֹב לַחֲסוֹת בַּיהוה מִבְּטֹחַ בִּנְדִיבִים.

עָזִּי וְזִמְרָת יָהּ וַיְהִי־לִי לִישׁוּעָה.

קוֹל רִנָּה וִישׁוּעָה בְּאָהֳלֵי צַדִּיקִים. יְמִין יהוה עֹשָׂה חָיִל.

יְמִין יהוה רוֹמֵמָה; יְמִין יהוה עֹשָׂה חָיִל.

לֹא אָמוּת כִּי־אֶחְיֶה וַאֲסַפֵּר מַעֲשֵׂי יָהּ.

פִּתְחוּ־לִי שַׁעֲרֵי־צֶדֶק; אָבֹא־בָם אוֹדֶה יָהּ.

זֶה־הַשַּׁעַר לַיהוה; צַדִּיקִים יָבֹאוּ בוֹ.

אוֹדְךָ כִּי עֲנִיתָנִי וַתְּהִי־לִי לִישׁוּעָה.

אֶבֶן מָאֲסוּ הַבּוֹנִים הָיְתָה לְרֹאשׁ פִּנָּה.

מֵאֵת יהוה הָיְתָה זֹּאת; הִיא נִפְלָאת בְּעֵינֵינוּ.

זֶה־הַיּוֹם עָשָׂה יהוה נָגִילָה וְנִשְׂמְחָה בוֹ.

It is better to take refuge in God than to rely on human beings.
It is better to take refuge in God than to rely on those in power.

God is my strength and my shield,
and has become my salvation.

Hear! Glad songs of triumph in the tents of the righteous!
The Eternal One does mighty deeds.
God's power is supreme;
The Eternal One does mighty deeds.

I shall not die, but live to tell of God's deeds.
Open for me the gates of righteousness;
let me enter them and give thanks to God.

This is the gate of the Eternal One; the righteous shall enter it.
I thank You, for You have answered me, and become my salvation.

The stone that the builders rejected has become the chief cornerstone.
This is the work of the Eternal One; it is marvellous in our sight.

This is the day that God has made—
let us rejoice and be glad in it.

אָנָּא יהוה, הוֹשִׁיעָה נָּא!

אָנָּא יהוה, הוֹשִׁיעָה נָּא!

אָנָּא יהוה, הַצְלִיחָה נָּא!

אָנָּא יהוה, הַצְלִיחָה נָּא!

בָּרוּךְ הַבָּא בְּשֵׁם יהוה;

בֵּרַכְנוּכֶם מִבֵּית יהוה.

אֵלִי אַתָּה, וְאוֹדֶךָּ;

אֱלֹהַי, אֲרוֹמְמֶךָּ.

הוֹדוּ לַיהוה כִּי־טוֹב,

כִּי לְעוֹלָם חַסְדּוֹ.

Eternal God, deliver us!
Eternal God, deliver us!
Eternal God, prosper us!
Eternal God, prosper us!
Blessed are you who come in
God's name;
*here, in God's house, may you
be blessed.*
You are my God, and I thank You;
You are my God, I exalt You.
Give thanks to the Eternal
One, who is good,
whose love is everlasting.

ברכת השיר | Benediction of Song

יְהַלְלוּךָ, יי אֱלֹהֵינוּ, כָּל־מַעֲשֶׂיךָ; וַחֲסִידֶיךָ, צַדִּיקִים
עוֹשֵׂי רְצוֹנֶךָ, וְכָל־עַמְּךָ בֵּית יִשְׂרָאֵל, בְּרִנָּה יוֹדוּ
וִיבָרְכוּ, וִישַׁבְּחוּ וִיפָאֲרוּ וִירוֹמְמוּ וְיַעֲרִיצוּ, וְיַקְדִּישׁוּ
וְיַמְלִיכוּ אֶת־שִׁמְךָ, מַלְכֵּנוּ. כִּי לְךָ טוֹב לְהוֹדוֹת,
וּלְשִׁמְךָ נָאֶה לְזַמֵּר, כִּי מֵעוֹלָם וְעַד עוֹלָם אַתָּה אֵל.
בָּרוּךְ אַתָּה יי מֶלֶךְ מְהֻלָּל בַּתִּשְׁבָּחוֹת.

When the freedom they wished for most was freedom from responsibility, then Athens ceased to be free and was never free again.
—Edith Hamilton

All Your works shall praise You, Eternal God,
giving thanks and praise to Your name.
It is good to thank You, right to sing Your praises,
for You are God now and always, to the end of time.

נִשְׁמַת כָּל־חַי תְּבָרֵךְ אֶת־שִׁמְךָ, יי אֱלֹהֵינוּ, וְרוּחַ
כָּל־בָּשָׂר תְּפָאֵר וּתְרוֹמֵם זִכְרְךָ, מַלְכֵּנוּ תָּמִיד.
מִן הָעוֹלָם וְעַד־הָעוֹלָם אַתָּה אֵל. אֱלֹהֵי הָרִאשׁוֹנִים
וְהָאַחֲרוֹנִים, אֱלוֹהַּ כָּל־בְּרִיּוֹת, אֲדוֹן כָּל־תּוֹלָדוֹת,
הַמְהֻלָּל בְּרֹב הַתִּשְׁבָּחוֹת, הַמְנַהֵג עוֹלָמוֹ בְּחֶסֶד
וּבְרִיּוֹתָיו בְּרַחֲמִים. לְךָ לְבַדְּךָ אֲנַחְנוּ מוֹדִים.

The soul of every living being shall praise Your name, Eternal
One, our God, and the spirit of all flesh shall acclaim Your majesty
forever. From everlasting to everlasting You are God.

God of all ages, of all generations, of all creatures, to whom our
praise ascends: You guide the world with constant love, Your children
with tender care. To You alone we give thanks.

אִלּוּ פִינוּ מָלֵא שִׁירָה כַּיָּם, וּלְשׁוֹנֵנוּ כַּהֲמוֹן גַּלָּיו,
וְשִׂפְתוֹתֵינוּ שֶׁבַח כְּמֶרְחֲבֵי רָקִיעַ, וְעֵינֵינוּ מְאִירוֹת
כַּשֶּׁמֶשׁ וְכַיָּרֵחַ, וְיָדֵינוּ פְרוּשׂוֹת כְּנִשְׁרֵי שָׁמָיִם, וְרַגְלֵינוּ
קַלּוֹת כָּאַיָּלוֹת–אֵין אֲנַחְנוּ מַסְפִּיקִים לְהוֹדוֹת לְךָ, וּלְבָרֵךְ
אֶת־שִׁמְךָ, עַל־אַחַת מֵאֶלֶף, אֶלֶף אַלְפֵי אֲלָפִים וְרִבֵּי רְבָבוֹת
פְּעָמִים הַטּוֹבוֹת שֶׁעָשִׂיתָ עִם־אֲבוֹתֵינוּ וְאִמּוֹתֵינוּ וְעִמָּנוּ.
עַל כֵּן אֵבָרִים שֶׁפִּלַּגְתָּ בָּנוּ, וְרוּחַ וּנְשָׁמָה שֶׁנָּפַחְתָּ בְּאַפֵּינוּ,
וְלָשׁוֹן אֲשֶׁר שַׂמְתָּ בְּפִינוּ, הֵן הֵם יוֹדוּ וִיבָרְכוּ וִישַׁבְּחוּ

וִיפָאֲרוּ אֶת־שִׁמְךָ, מַלְכֵּנוּ.

כִּי כָל־פֶּה לְךָ יוֹדֶה,

וְכָל־לָשׁוֹן לְךָ תִּשָּׁבַע,

וְכָל־בֶּרֶךְ לְךָ תִכְרַע,

וְכָל־קוֹמָה לְפָנֶיךָ תִשְׁתַּחֲוֶה,

וְכָל־לְבָבוֹת יִירָאוּךָ,

וְכָל־קֶרֶב וּכְלָיוֹת יְזַמְּרוּ לִשְׁמֶךָ.

כַּדָּבָר שֶׁכָּתוּב: כָּל־עַצְמוֹתַי תֹּאמַרְנָה: יי, מִי כָמְוֹךָ?

נְהַלֶּךְ וּנְשַׁבֵּחַךְ וּנְפָאֶרְךָ וּנְבָרֶךְ אֶת־שֵׁם קָדְשֶׁךָ,

כָּאָמוּר: בָּרְכִי, נַפְשִׁי, אֶת־יי, וְכָל־קְרָבַי אֶת־שֵׁם קָדְשׁוֹ!

Yet though our mouths should overflow with song as the sea, our tongues with exultation as the roaring waves, and our lips with praise as heaven's wide expanse; and though our eyes shine as the sun and moon, our arms spread forth like the wings of eagles, and our feet speed swiftly as hinds'—still we could not fully thank You, Eternal One, our God, for Your infinite kindness to our ancestors and to us.

Therefore the limbs You have formed in us,
the spirit You have breathed into us,
and the tongue You have set in our mouths:
all shall unite to thank and praise You,
extol You and exalt You,
the sovereign God.

Every mouth shall thank You,
every tongue bear witness to You.
Every knee shall bend to You,
every body bow down to You.
Every heart shall revere You,
and every fibre of our being shall sing Your praise.

For so it is written: All my bones shall say: Who is like You, Eternal One? Therefore we extol You, and proclaim Your glory, and praise Your holy name, as it is said: Praise the Eternal One, O my soul; let all that is within me praise God's holy name.

A people may prefer a free government, but if, from indolence, or carelessness, or cowardice... they are unequal to the exertions necessary for preserving it; if they will not fight for it when it is directly attacked; if they can be deluded by the artifices used to cheat them out of it; if by momentary discouragement, or temporary panic, or a fit of enthusiasm for an individual, they can be induced to lay their liberties at the feet even of a great man, or trust him with powers which enable him to subvert their institutions; in all these cases they are more or less unfit for liberty: and... they are unlikely long to enjoy it.

—John Stuart Mill

כוס של אליהו | The Cup of Elijah

The cups are refilled. If desired, the Cup of Elijah is passed around, with each person pouring a little wine into that cup.

The door is opened

Leader:

Why do we drink four cups of wine at this service? Our tradition is rich in answers:

A Reader:

Each cup stands for the promise of freedom. We drink four cups to say: let freedom reign in the four corners of the earth.

A Reader:

They are the four seasons. We drink the four cups to say: let freedom reign in every season of the year.

A Reader:

They are the "four empires" that oppressed us in days of old. We drink the four cups to say: let tyranny pass away, let all the world be free.

A Reader:

And we drink the four cups in remembrance of the four divine promises of redemption. As it is said: Say then to the people of Israel:

All:

I am the Eternal One, and
I will BRING YOU OUT from under the Egyptian yoke.
I will DELIVER YOU from their bondage,
I will REDEEM YOU with outstretched arm.
I will TAKE YOU to be My people. ...

Leader:

But there is a fifth promise: "… and I will BRING YOU INTO the land…." Should there then be a Fifth Cup? That question, says tradition, will not be answered until Elijah comes to proclaim the Messianic Time. Meanwhile it is a promise we remember with a cup from which we cannot drink, until all the world is redeemed from pain, injustice, denial of love. When will that time come?

A Reader:

The world is far from redemption. Our story, we have said, begins with degradation and ends with glory. Pain, injustice, denial of love: since our beginning we have known many degradations.

A Leader:

בְּכָל־דּוֹר וָדוֹר עוֹמְדִים
עָלֵינוּ לְכַלּוֹתֵנוּ . . .

In every generation there are those who seek to destroy us …

A Reader:

וְהַקָּדוֹשׁ בָּרוּךְ הוּא מַצִּילֵנוּ
מִיָּדָם.

V'ha-ka-dosh Ba-ruch Hu
ma-tzi-lei-nu mi-ya-dam.

But the Holy One saves us from their hands.

A Reader:

We remember expulsions and ghettos and inquisition.

A Reader:

We remember forced conversions and pogroms, enslavement and exile.

A Reader:

We remember the camps, a nightmare planet where one third of our people were reduced to ash.

All:

כִּי אָכַל אֶת־יַעֲקֹב, וְאֶת־נָוֵהוּ הֵשַׁמּוּ.

They have devoured Jacob and laid waste our dwelling-places.

A Reader:

וְהַקָּדוֹשׁ בָּרוּךְ הוּא הִצִּלָנוּ מִיָּדָם!

But we have saved the Holy One from their hands!

A Reader:

For from these fugitives, these oppressed, these martyrs came deeds of justice, and love, and truth. They are the people of Torah, children of the prophets; their forebears wrote Psalms of Praise.

All:

We shall remember. We shall not forget.
Praised is the one who remembers the glory!
Praised is the one who lingers over the telling!

A Reader:

We remember many glories: we have married and raised children. We have sung God's praises. We have worked and rested, loved and laughed. The very land for which we braved the wilderness, in which we made our home: to that same land our people have returned, to build and be rebuilt.

All:

שָׁמְעָה וַתִּשְׂמַח צִיּוֹן;
וַתָּגֵלְנָה בְּנוֹת יְהוּדָה.

Zion heard and was glad; the daughters of Judah rejoiced.

A Reader:

But the full glory is still far from sight. Ignorance, prejudice, hatred; contempt for truth and justice; hunger and terror; war and the fear of war: these remain to plague the human race.

To end these plagues, to summon Elijah—that is the task of all who care. It is our task, for we are the people who know the stranger's heart, the slave's aching bones, the shaking hands of the exile. When will Elijah come with the news of freedom? When we have called him by our deeds. Then we shall say:

All:

כּוֹס־יְשׁוּעוֹת אֶשָּׂא, וּבְשֵׁם
יהוה אֶקְרָא.

*I will lift up the cup of salvation,
and call upon the name of God.*

Leader:

Again, and yet again, we look into the future with a question on our lips and in our hearts. When shall we find answers that do not puzzle us? Where shall we find a drink that does not make us thirst all the more for having swallowed it?

A Reader:

Tonight we have asked questions and recited answers, although we know that every answer becomes a new question. For we know too that each new question may lead us to another answer.

A Reader:

In the lore of our people one figure stands for all who have these two gifts: the gift of asking a question, the gift of listening to an answer.

A Reader:

Elijah, who challenged power with the question of justice. (*I Kings 21*)

A Reader:

Elijah, whose own question to God found its answer in a still, small voice whispering within him. (*I Kings 19*)

A Reader:

Elijah, herald of reconciliation in time to come, when questions and answers shall flow among us. In our love, we shall come to understand. Then our redemption shall begin. As it is written:

All:

הִנֵּה אָנֹכִי שֹׁלֵחַ לָכֶם אֵת אֵלִיָּהוּ הַנָּבִיא
לִפְנֵי בּוֹא יוֹם יהוה הַגָּדוֹל וְהַנּוֹרָא:
וְהֵשִׁיב לֵב־אָבוֹת עַל־בָּנִים, וְלֵב בָּנִים עַל־אֲבוֹתָם.

"Behold, I am sending to you Elijah the prophet before the coming of the great and awesome day of the Eternal One: to turn the hearts of parents to their children, and the hearts of children to their parents."

Leader:

And ON THAT DAY the promise of promises shall be fulfilled. As it is written:

All:

וְהֵבֵאתִי אֶתְכֶם אֶל
הָאָרֶץ . . . .

V'HEI-VEI-TI et-chem el ha-a-retz. ...

And I will BRING YOU INTO the land. ... (Exodus 6:8)

A Reader:

Israel and all the world shall reach the Land of Promise.

All:

SPEEDILY, IN OUR DAYS. AMEN.

The door is closed

p. 98

All:

אֵלִיָּהוּ הַנָּבִיא, אֵלִיָּהוּ
הַתִּשְׁבִּי, אֵלִיָּהוּ, אֵלִיָּהוּ,
אֵלִיָּהוּ הַגִּלְעָדִי.
בִּמְהֵרָה בְיָמֵינוּ, יָבֹא אֵלֵינוּ,
עִם מָשִׁיחַ בֶּן דָּוִד,
עִם מָשִׁיחַ בֶּן דָּוִד.
אֵלִיָּהוּ ...

Ei-li-ya-hu ha-na-vi, Eiliyahu
ha-tish-bi; Ei-li-ya-hu, Ei-li-ya-hu,
Ei-li-ya-hu ha-gil-adi.
Bi-m'hei-ra v'ya-mei-nu, ya-vo
ei-lei-nu; im ma-shi-ach ben
Da-vid, im ma-shi-ach ben
Da-vid.
Ei-li-ya-hu ha–na-vi…

Rabbi Yehoshua once came upon the prophet Elijah at the entrance of the cave of Rabbi Shimon bar Yochai. Yehoshua asked:

When will the Messiah come? Go ask him, said the prophet.

He sits at the gates of Rome, like all the poor. His body is covered with running sores, as is theirs. This is how you can tell him apart from them: When they want to apply fresh bandages, the others first remove all the old dressings. Not so with him—he never changes more than one dressing at a time, for he thinks: I must be ready to answer the call without delay!

Rabbi Yehoshua went to Rome's gates and found him. He said: Shalom to you, Master and Teacher! The reply was: Shalom to you, Son of Levi! Yehoshua then asked: Master, when are you coming?

And the answer was: Today!

Yehoshua left with a full heart, and returned to his place. But the day passed, and with the fall of eve no change could be seen.

Yehoshua turned to Elijah and wept: The Messiah lied! Today! he said, yet he did not come… . But Elijah said: You must understand what he meant. Is it not written?

"Today—if you will but listen to God's voice." (Psalm 95:7) (Talmud)

נרצה | Conclusion

Leader:

Our celebration must not end before we remember our duty to remember. As it is said:

וְשָׂמַחְתָּ לִפְנֵי יהוה אֱלֹהֶיךָ: אַתָּה, וּבִנְךָ, וּבִתֶּךָ, וְהַגֵּר,
וְהַיָּתוֹם, וְהָאַלְמָנָה אֲשֶׁר בְּקִרְבֶּךָ,

"As you rejoice before your Eternal God—you, your son and daughter, the stranger, the orphan, and the widow in your midst—

All:

וְזָכַרְתָּ כִּי־עֶבֶד הָיִיתָ בְּמִצְרָיִם.

"Remember that you were a slave in the land of Egypt."

Leader:

May our remembering lead to acts of love and kindness, for we know the ache in the stranger's heart:

All:

כְּאֶזְרָח מִכֶּם יִהְיֶה לָכֶם הַגֵּר הַגָּר אִתְּכֶם,
וְאָהַבְתָּ לוֹ כָּמוֹךָ, כִּי־גֵרִים הֱיִיתֶם בְּאֶרֶץ מִצְרָיִם.

"The strangers in your midst shall be to you as the native-born, and you shall love them as yourselves, for you were strangers in the land of Egypt."

Leader:

There shall be among us neither master nor slave, as it is said:

All:

כִּי־לִי בְנֵי־יִשְׂרָאֵל עֲבָדִים: עֲבָדַי הֵם, אֲשֶׁר הוֹצֵאתִי אוֹתָם
מֵאֶרֶץ מִצְרָיִם. אֲנִי יהוה אֱלֹהֵיכֶם.

"Only Me shall the people of Israel serve; they are My servants whom I brought out of the land of Egypt; I am your Eternal God."

כוס רביעי | The Fourth Cup

To be at one, finally: with oneself, one's friends and neighbors, one's people, is to achieve the fourth promise: to be at one with God.

Leader:

Our redemption is not yet complete, but as we raise the final cup of wine in remembrance of the fourth promise of redemption, our hearts beat strong with hope. For it is said:

All:

וְלָקַחְתִּי אֶתְכֶם לִי לְעָם, וְהָיִיתִי לָכֶם לֵאלֹהִים.

V'LA-KACH-TI et-chem li l'am, v'ha-yi-ti la-chem lei-lo-him.
I will TAKE YOU to be My people, and I will be your God.

בָּרוּךְ אַתָּה יי אֱלֹהֵינוּ מֶלֶךְ הָעוֹלָם, בּוֹרֵא פְּרִי הַגָּפֶן.

Ba-ruch a-ta Adonai, Eh-lo-hei-nu meh-lech ha-o-lam, bo-rei p'ri ha-ga-fen.

We praise You, Eternal One, for the fruit of the vine.

בָּרוּךְ אַתָּה יי אֱלֹהֵינוּ מֶלֶךְ הָעוֹלָם, שֶׁעָשָׂנוּ בְּנֵי וּבְנוֹת חוֹרִין.

Ba-ruch a-ta Adonai, Eh-lo-hei-nu meh-lech ha-o-lam, sheh-a-sa-nu b'nei u'v'not cho-rin.

We praise You, Eternal One: You have made us to be free.

All now drink the fourth cup

Courtesy of Sotheby's

Leader:

חֲסַל סִדּוּר פֶּסַח   Our Seder now concludes,

כְּהִלְכָתוֹ,   its rites and customs done.

כְּכָל־מִשְׁפָּטוֹ   This year's task completed,

וְחֻקָּתוֹ.   we look to a time yet unborn.

כַּאֲשֶׁר זָכִינוּ   We look to the light of dawn,

לְסַדֵּר אוֹתוֹ,   tomorrow's promised Passover,

כֵּן נִזְכֶּה   the days of peace, the days of love,

לַעֲשׂוֹתוֹ.   the time of full redemption.

All:

Tomorrow's promised Passover:
the days of peace,
the days of love,
the time of full redemption.

Leader:

Then all shall sit under their vines and under their fig-trees,
and none shall make them afraid.

All:

לָנוּ וּלְכָל־בֵּית יִשְׂרָאֵל

לָנוּ וּלְכָל־יוֹשְׁבֵי תֵבֵל׃

לַשָּׁנָה הַבָּאָה בִּירוּשָׁלָיִם!

לַשָּׁנָה הַבָּאָה

כָּל־חַי נִגְאָל!

FOR US AND ALL ISRAEL,
FOR US AND ALL HUMANKIND:
NEXT YEAR IN JERUSALEM!
NEXT YEAR
ALL THE WORLD REDEEMED!

פרקי שירה | Poems and Songs

The seder concludes with songs. Our selection makes available some traditional songs from Medieval times, some songs from modern Israel, and one or two others. The Hebrew of our first two selections is in the form of an alphahabetical acrostic: appropriately playful for the occasion. We provide acrostics in the English, too.

KI LO NA-EH

כִּי לוֹ נָאֶה, כִּי לוֹ יָאֶה.
אַדִּיר בִּמְלוּכָה, בָּחוּר
כַּהֲלָכָה, גְּדוּדָיו יֹאמְרוּ לוֹ:
לְךָ וּלְךָ, לְךָ כִּי לְךָ, לְךָ
אַף לְךָ, לְךָ יְיָ הַמַּמְלָכָה.
כִּי לוֹ נָאֶה, כִּי לוֹ יָאֶה.

דָּגוּל בִּמְלוּכָה, הָדוּר
כַּהֲלָכָה,וָתִיקָיו יֹאמְרוּ לוֹ:
לְךָ וּלְךָ, לְךָ כִּי לְךָ, לְךָ
אַף לְךָ, לְךָ יְיָ הַמַּמְלָכָה.
כִּי לוֹ נָאֶה, כִּי לוֹ יָאֶה.

זַכַּאי בִּמְלוּכָה, חָסִין
כַּהֲלָכָה, טַפְסְרָיו יֹאמְרוּ לוֹ:
לְךָ וּלְךָ, לְךָ כִּי לְךָ, לְךָ
אַף לְךָ, לְךָ יְיָ הַמַּמְלָכָה.
כִּי לוֹ נָאֶה, כִּי לוֹ יָאֶה.

יָחִיד בִּמְלוּכָה, כַּבִּיר
כַּהֲלָכָה, לִמּוּדָיו יֹאמְרוּ לוֹ:
לְךָ וּלְךָ, לְךָ כִּי לְךָ, לְךָ
אַף לְךָ, לְךָ יְיָ הַמַּמְלָכָה.
כִּי לוֹ נָאֶה, כִּי לוֹ יָאֶה.

מָרוֹם בִּמְלוּכָה, נוֹרָא
כַּהֲלָכָה, סְבִיבָיו יֹאמְרוּ לוֹ:
לְךָ וּלְךָ, לְךָ כִּי לְךָ, לְךָ
אַף לְךָ, לְךָ יְיָ הַמַּמְלָכָה.
כִּי לוֹ נָאֶה, כִּי לוֹ יָאֶה.

Ki lo na-eh, ki lo ya-eh.
Adir bim-lu-cha, Bachur ka-halacha,
G'dudav yo-m'ru lo:
l'cha u-l'cha, l'cha ki l'cha, l'cha af l'cha,
l'cha Adonai ha-mam-la-cha.
Ki lo na-eh, ki lo ya-eh.

Dagul bim-lu-cha, Hadur ka-halacha,
Vatikav yo-m'ru lo:
l'cha u-l'cha, l'cha ki l'cha, l'cha af l'cha,
l'cha Adonai ha-mam-la-cha.
Ki lo na-eh, ki lo ya-eh.

Zakai bim-lu-cha, Cha-sin ka-halacha,
Taf-s'rav yo-m'ru lo:
l'cha u-l'cha, l'cha ki l'cha, l'cha af l'cha,
l'cha Adonai ha-mam-la-cha.
Ki lo na-eh, ki lo ya-eh.

Yachid bim-lu-cha, Kabir ka-halacha,
Limudav yo-m'ru lo:
l'cha u-l'cha, l'cha ki l'cha, l'cha af l'cha,
l'cha Adonai ha-mam-la-cha.
Ki lo na-eh, ki lo ya-eh.

Marom bim-lu-cha, Nora ka-halacha,
S'vivav yo-m'ru lo:
l'cha u-l'cha, l'cha ki l'cha, l'cha af l'cha,
l'cha Adonai ha-mam-la-cha.
Ki lo na-eh, ki lo ya-eh.

עָנָיו בִּמְלוּכָה, פּוֹדֶה
כַּהֲלָכָה, צַדִּיקָיו יֹאמְרוּ לוֹ:
לְךָ וּלְךָ, לְךָ כִּי לְךָ, לְךָ
אַף לְךָ, לְךָ יי הַמַּמְלָכָה.
כִּי לוֹ נָאֶה, כִּי לוֹ יָאֶה.

קָדוֹשׁ בִּמְלוּכָה, רַחוּם
כַּהֲלָכָה, שִׁנְאַנָּיו יֹאמְרוּ לוֹ:
לְךָ וּלְךָ, לְךָ כִּי לְךָ, לְךָ
אַף לְךָ, לְךָ יי הַמַּמְלָכָה.
כִּי לוֹ נָאֶה, כִּי לוֹ יָאֶה.

תַּקִּיף בִּמְלוּכָה, תּוֹמֵךְ
כַּהֲלָכָה, תְּמִימָיו יֹאמְרוּ לוֹ:
לְךָ וּלְךָ, לְךָ כִּי לְךָ, לְךָ
אַף לְךָ, לְךָ יי הַמַּמְלָכָה.
כִּי לוֹ נָאֶה, כִּי לוֹ יָאֶה.

Anav bim-lu-cha, Podeh ka-halacha,
Tza-di-kav yo-m'ru lo:
l'cha u-l'cha, l'cha ki l'cha, l'cha af l'cha,
l'cha Adonai ha-mam-la-cha.
Ki lo na-eh, ki lo ya-eh.

Kadosh bim-lu-cha, Rachum ka-halacha,
Shin-anav yo-m'ru lo:
l'cha u-l'cha, l'cha ki l'cha, l'cha af l'cha,
l'cha Adonai ha-mam-la-cha.
Ki lo na-eh, ki lo ya-eh.

Takif bim-lu-cha, Tomeich ka-halacha,
T'mi-mav yo-m'ru lo:
l'cha u-l'cha, l'cha ki l'cha, l'cha af l'cha,
l'cha Adonai ha-mam-la-cha.
Ki lo na-eh, ki lo ya-eh.

To You praise belongs;
to You praise is due.

Almighty in rule,
Beloved by right,
Your Chosen ones sing:
Yours only, Yours solely,
Yours alone, God,
is the dominion.
To You praise belongs,
to You praise is due.

Dominant in rule,
Excelling by right,
Your Faithful ones sing:
Yours only....

Glorious in rule,
Hallowed by right,
Your just ones sing:
Yours only....

Kindly in rule,
Lawgiver by right,
Your Ministers sing:
Yours only....

Nonpareil in rule,
Omnipresent by right,
Your People sing:
Yours only....

Resplendent in Rule,
Sovereign by right,
Your Thankful ones sing:
Yours only....

Unrivaled in rule,
Your Worshippers sing:
Yours only....

Worthy of rule,
Wonderful by right,
Your Witnesses sing:
Yours only....

ADIR HU

אַדִּיר הוּא, אַדִּיר הוּא,
יִגְאָלֵנוּ בְּקָרוֹב,
בִּמְהֵרָה, בִּמְהֵרָה,
בְּיָמֵינוּ בְּקָרוֹב.
אֵל פְּדֵה, אֵל פְּדֵה,
פְּדֵה עַמְּךָ בְּקָרוֹב.

Adir hu (2), yig-a-lei-nu b'karov,
bi-m'hei-ra, bi-m'hei-ra
b'ya-mei-nu b'ka-rov. El p'dei,
El p'dei, p'dei a-m'cha b'ka-rov.

בָּחוּר הוּא, גָּדוֹל הוּא,
דָּגוּל הוּא, יִגְאָלֵנוּ בְּקָרוֹב,
בִּמְהֵרָה, בִּמְהֵרָה, בְּיָמֵינוּ
בְּקָרוֹב.
אֵל פְּדֵה, אֵל פְּדֵה,
פְּדֵה עַמְּךָ בְּקָרוֹב.

Ba-chur hu, ga-dol hu, Da-gul
hu, yig-a-lei-nu b'karov,
bi-m'hei-ra, bi-m'hei-ra
b'ya-mei-nu b'ka-rov. El p'dei,
El p'dei, p'dei a-m'cha b'ka-rov.

הָדוּר הוּא, וָתִיק הוּא,
זַכַּאי הוּא, יִגְאָלֵנוּ בְּקָרוֹב
בִּמְהֵרָה, בִּמְהֵרָה, בְּיָמֵינוּ
בְּקָרוֹב.
אֵל פְּדֵה, אֵל פְּדֵה,
פְּדֵה עַמְּךָ בְּקָרוֹב.

Ha-dur hu, va-tik hu,
za-ki hu, yig-a-lei-nu b'ka-rov
bi-m'hei-ra, bi-m'hei-ra
b'ya-mei-nu b'ka-rov El p'dei,
El p'dei, p'dei a-m'cha b'ka-rov.

חָסִיד הוּא, טָהוֹר הוּא,
יָחִיד הוּא, יִגְאָלֵנוּ בְּקָרוֹב,
בִּמְהֵרָה, בִּמְהֵרָה, בְּיָמֵינוּ
בְּקָרוֹב.
אֵל פְּדֵה, אֵל פְּדֵה,
פְּדֵה עַמְּךָ בְּקָרוֹב.

Cha-sid hu, Ta-hor hu, Ya-chid
hu, yig-a-lei-nu b'karov,
bi-m'hei-ra, bi-m'hei-ra
b'ya-mei-nu b'ka-rov El p'dei,
El p'dei, p'dei a-m'cha b'ka-rov.

כַּבִּיר הוּא, לָמוּד הוּא,
מֶלֶךְ הוּא, יִגְאָלֵנוּ בְּקָרוֹב,
בִּמְהֵרָה, בִּמְהֵרָה, בְּיָמֵינוּ
בְּקָרוֹב.
אֵל פְּדֵה, אֵל פְּדֵה,
פְּדֵה עַמְּךָ בְּקָרוֹב.

Ka-bir hu, La-mud hu, Meh-lech
hu, yig-a-lei-nu b'karov,
bi-m'hei-ra, bi-m'hei-ra
b'ya-mei-nu b'ka-rov El p'dei,
El p'dei, p'dei a-m'cha b'ka-rov.

נוֹרָא הוּא, סַגִּיב הוּא,
עִזּוּז הוּא, יִגְאָלֵנוּ בְּקָרוֹב,
בִּמְהֵרָה, בִּמְהֵרָה, בְּיָמֵינוּ
בְּקָרוֹב.
אֵל פְּדֵה, אֵל פְּדֵה,
פְּדֵה עַמְּךָ בְּקָרוֹב.

No-ra hu, Sa-giv hu, I-zuz hu,
yig-a-lei-nu b'karov, bi-m'hei-ra,
bi-m'hei-ra b'ya-mei-nu
b'ka-rov El p'dei, El p'dei, p'dei
a-m'cha b'ka-rov.

p. 98

פּוֹדֶה הוּא, צַדִּיק הוּא,
קָדוֹשׁ הוּא, יִגְאָלֵנוּ בְּקָרוֹב,
בִּמְהֵרָה, בִּמְהֵרָה, בְּיָמֵינוּ
בְּקָרוֹב.
אֵל פְּדֵה, אֵל פְּדֵה,
פְּדֵה עַמְּךָ בְּקָרוֹב.

*Po-deh hu, Tza-dik hu, Kadosh
hu, yig-a-lei-nu b'karov,
bi-m'hei-ra, bi-m'hei-ra
b'ya-mei-nu b'ka-rov El p'dei,
El p'dei, p'dei a-m'cha b'ka-rov.*

רַחוּם הוּא, שַׁדַּי הוּא,
תַּקִּיף הוּא, יִגְאָלֵנוּ בְּקָרוֹב,
בִּמְהֵרָה, בִּמְהֵרָה, בְּיָמֵינוּ
בְּקָרוֹב.
אֵל פְּדֵה, אֵל פְּדֵה,
פְּדֵה עַמְּךָ בְּקָרוֹב.

*Ra-chum hu, Shaddai hu, Takif
hu, yig-a-lei-nu b'karov,
bi-m'hei-ra, bi-m'hei-ra
b'ya-mei-nu b'ka-rov El p'dei,
El p'dei, p'dei a-m'cha b'ka-rov.*

Awesome One (2), soon may You redeem us, speedily, speedily,
soon within our lifetime.
Save, O God; save, O God,
save Your people speedily.

Blessed One, Caring One, Devoted One,
soon may You redeem us…

Endless One, Faithful One, Gracious One,
soon may You redeem us…

Holy One, Infinite One, Joying One,
soon may You redeem us…

Knowing One, Loving One, Mighty One,
soon may You redeem us…

Noble One, Only One, Perfect One,
 soon may You redeem us…

Righteous One, Saving One, Teaching One
soon may You redeem us…

Unique One, Valiant One, Wisest One,
 soon may You redeem us…

GOD OF MIGHT

God of might, God of right,
Rock of our salvation,
Unto You still we do Offer adoration,
Since Your hand from Egypt's land
Led Your joyful nation.

God of all, when we call,
On Your love unending,
Save and hear; O be near,
Unto us extending
Power benign, grace divine
In our hearts descending.

Mighty God, by Your rod
Freedom first was given.
Now as then, let again
Bonds and chains be riven,
You our trust, wise and just,
God of earth and heaven.

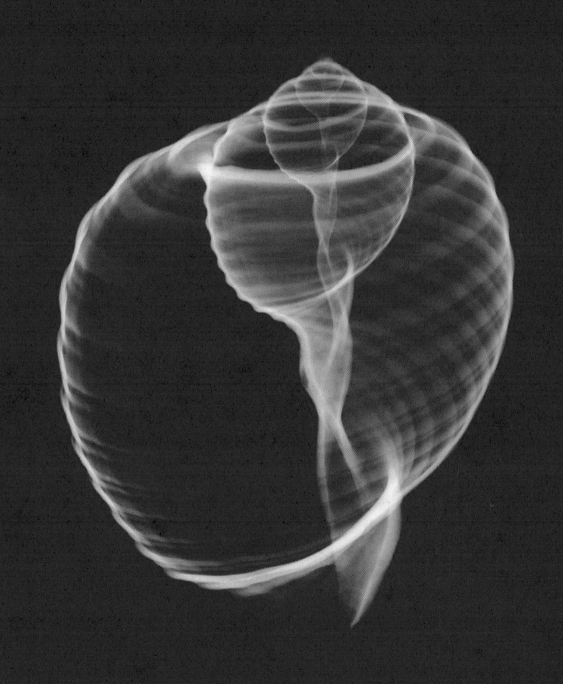

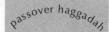

WHO KNOWS ONE?

This traditional riddle song goes from one to thirteen. The Hebrew word for One is echad, אחד; the numerical value of its three letters is—Thirteen…

p. 99

אֶחָד מִי יוֹדֵעַ? אֶחָד אֲנִי יוֹדֵעַ:

אֶחָד אֱלֹהֵינוּ שֶׁבַּשָּׁמַיִם וּבָאָרֶץ.

שְׁנַיִם מִי יוֹדֵעַ? שְׁנַיִם אֲנִי יוֹדֵעַ:

שְׁנֵי לֻחוֹת הַבְּרִית,

אֶחָד אֱלֹהֵינוּ שֶׁבַּשָּׁמַיִם וּבָאָרֶץ.

שְׁלֹשָׁה מִי יוֹדֵעַ? שְׁלֹשָׁה אֲנִי יוֹדֵעַ:

שְׁלֹשָׁה אָבוֹת, שְׁנֵי לֻחוֹת הַבְּרִית,

אֶחָד אֱלֹהֵינוּ שֶׁבַּשָּׁמַיִם וּבָאָרֶץ.

אַרְבַּע מִי יוֹדֵעַ? אַרְבַּע אֲנִי יוֹדֵעַ:

אַרְבַּע אִמָּהוֹת, שְׁלֹשָׁה אָבוֹת, שְׁנֵי לֻחוֹת הַבְּרִית,

אֶחָד אֱלֹהֵינוּ שֶׁבַּשָּׁמַיִם וּבָאָרֶץ.

חֲמִשָּׁה מִי יוֹדֵעַ? חֲמִשָּׁה אֲנִי יוֹדֵעַ:

חֲמִשָּׁה חֻמְשֵׁי תוֹרָה,

אַרְבַּע אִמָּהוֹת, שְׁלֹשָׁה אָבוֹת, שְׁנֵי לֻחוֹת הַבְּרִית,

אֶחָד אֱלֹהֵינוּ שֶׁבַּשָּׁמַיִם וּבָאָרֶץ.

שִׁשָּׁה מִי יוֹדֵעַ? שִׁשָּׁה אֲנִי יוֹדֵעַ:

שִׁשָּׁה סִדְרֵי מִשְׁנָה, חֲמִשָּׁה חֻמְשֵׁי תוֹרָה,

אַרְבַּע אִמָּהוֹת, שְׁלֹשָׁה אָבוֹת, שְׁנֵי לֻחוֹת הַבְּרִית,

אֶחָד אֱלֹהֵינוּ שֶׁבַּשָּׁמַיִם וּבָאָרֶץ.

שִׁבְעָה מִי יוֹדֵעַ? שִׁבְעָה אֲנִי יוֹדֵעַ:

שִׁבְעָה יְמֵי שַׁבַּתָּא, שִׁשָּׁה סִדְרֵי מִשְׁנָה, חֲמִשָּׁה חֻמְשֵׁי תוֹרָה,

אַרְבַּע אִמָּהוֹת, שְׁלֹשָׁה אָבוֹת, שְׁנֵי לֻחוֹת הַבְּרִית,

אֶחָד אֱלֹהֵינוּ שֶׁבַּשָּׁמַיִם וּבָאָרֶץ.

שְׁמוֹנָה מִי יוֹדֵעַ? שְׁמוֹנָה אֲנִי יוֹדֵעַ:

שְׁמוֹנָה יְמֵי מִילָה,

שִׁבְעָה יְמֵי שַׁבַּתָּא, שִׁשָּׁה סִדְרֵי מִשְׁנָה, חֲמִשָּׁה חֻמְשֵׁי תוֹרָה,

אַרְבַּע אִמָּהוֹת, שְׁלֹשָׁה אָבוֹת, שְׁנֵי לֻחוֹת הַבְּרִית,

אֶחָד אֱלֹהֵינוּ שֶׁבַּשָּׁמַיִם וּבָאָרֶץ.

תִּשְׁעָה מִי יוֹדֵעַ? תִּשְׁעָה אֲנִי יוֹדֵעַ:

תִּשְׁעָה יַרְחֵי לֵדָה, שְׁמוֹנָה יְמֵי מִילָה,

שִׁבְעָה יְמֵי שַׁבַּתָּא, שִׁשָּׁה סִדְרֵי מִשְׁנָה, חֲמִשָּׁה חֻמְשֵׁי תוֹרָה,

אַרְבַּע אִמָּהוֹת, שְׁלֹשָׁה אָבוֹת, שְׁנֵי לֻחוֹת הַבְּרִית,

אֶחָד אֱלֹהֵינוּ שֶׁבַּשָּׁמַיִם וּבָאָרֶץ.

עֲשָׂרָה מִי יוֹדֵעַ? עֲשָׂרָה אֲנִי יוֹדֵעַ:

עֲשָׂרָה דִבְּרַיָּא, תִּשְׁעָה יַרְחֵי לֵדָה, שְׁמוֹנָה יְמֵי מִילָה,

שִׁבְעָה יְמֵי שַׁבַּתָּא, שִׁשָּׁה סִדְרֵי מִשְׁנָה, חֲמִשָּׁה חֻמְשֵׁי תוֹרָה,

אַרְבַּע אִמָּהוֹת, שְׁלֹשָׁה אָבוֹת, שְׁנֵי לֻחוֹת הַבְּרִית,

אֶחָד אֱלֹהֵינוּ שֶׁבַּשָּׁמַיִם וּבָאָרֶץ.

אַחַד עָשָׂר מִי יוֹדֵעַ? אַחַד עָשָׂר אֲנִי יוֹדֵעַ:

אַחַד עָשָׂר כּוֹכְבַיָּא, עֲשָׂרָה דִבְּרַיָּא, תִּשְׁעָה יַרְחֵי לֵדָה,

שְׁמוֹנָה יְמֵי מִילָה, שִׁבְעָה יְמֵי שַׁבַּתָּא, שִׁשָּׁה סִדְרֵי מִשְׁנָה,

חֲמִשָּׁה חֻמְשֵׁי תוֹרָה, אַרְבַּע אִמָּהוֹת, שְׁלֹשָׁה אָבוֹת,

שְׁנֵי לֻחוֹת הַבְּרִית,

אֶחָד אֱלֹהֵינוּ שֶׁבַּשָּׁמַיִם וּבָאָרֶץ.

שְׁנֵים עָשָׂר מִי יוֹדֵעַ? שְׁנֵים עָשָׂר אֲנִי יוֹדֵעַ:

שְׁנֵים עָשָׂר שִׁבְטַיָּא,

אַחַד עָשָׂר כּוֹכְבַיָּא, עֲשָׂרָה דִבְּרַיָּא, תִּשְׁעָה יַרְחֵי לֵדָה,

שְׁמוֹנָה יְמֵי מִילָה, שִׁבְעָה יְמֵי שַׁבַּתָּא, שִׁשָּׁה סִדְרֵי מִשְׁנָה,

חֲמִשָּׁה חֻמְשֵׁי תוֹרָה, אַרְבַּע אִמָּהוֹת, שְׁלֹשָׁה אָבוֹת,

שְׁנֵי לֻחוֹת הַבְּרִית,

אֶחָד אֱלֹהֵינוּ שֶׁבַּשָּׁמַיִם וּבָאָרֶץ.

שְׁלֹשָׁה עָשָׂר מִי יוֹדֵעַ? שְׁלֹשָׁה עָשָׂר אֲנִי יוֹדֵעַ:

שְׁלֹשָׁה עָשָׂר מִדַּיָּא, שְׁנֵים עָשָׂר שִׁבְטַיָּא,

אַחַד עָשָׂר כּוֹכְבַיָּא, עֲשָׂרָה דִבְּרַיָּא, תִּשְׁעָה יַרְחֵי לֵדָה,

שְׁמוֹנָה יְמֵי מִילָה, שִׁבְעָה יְמֵי שַׁבַּתָּא, שִׁשָּׁה סִדְרֵי מִשְׁנָה,

חֲמִשָּׁה חֻמְשֵׁי תוֹרָה, אַרְבַּע אִמָּהוֹת, שְׁלֹשָׁה אָבוֹת,

שְׁנֵי לֻחוֹת הַבְּרִית,

אֶחָד אֱלֹהֵינוּ שֶׁבַּשָּׁמַיִם וּבָאָרֶץ.

WHO CAN TELL ME OF THE NUMBER ONE?

Who can tell me of the number One? I can tell you of the number One.

One is almighty God, almighty God, almighty God, almighty God, who reigns in heaven and upon the earth, who reigns in heaven and upon the earth.

Who can tell me of the number two? I can tell you of the number two.

Two tables of the Law, One is almighty God, almighty God, almighty God, almighty God, who reigns in heaven and upon the earth, who reigns in heaven and upon the earth.

Who can tell me of the number three? I can tell you of the number three.

Three is the Patriarchs, Two tables of the Law, One is almighty God, almighty God, almighty God, almighty God, who reigns in heaven. …

Who can tell me of the number four? I can tell you of the number four.

Four is the Matriarchs, Three is the Patriarchs, Two tables of the Law, One is almighty God, almighty God. …

Who can tell me of the number five? I can tell you of the number five.

Five books of Moses, Four is the Matriarchs, Three is the Patriarchs, Two tables of the Law, One is almighty God, almighty God. …

Who can tell me of the number six? I can tell you of the number six.

Six are the Mishnah's Orders, Five books of Moses, Four is the Matriarchs, Three is the Patriarchs, Two tables of the Law, One is almighty God, almighty God. …

Who can tell me of the number seven? I can tell you of the number seven.

Seven days make up a week, Six are the Mishnah's Orders, Five books of Moses, Four is the Matriarchs, Three is the Patriarchs, Two tables of the Law, One is almighty God. …

Who can tell me of the number eight? I can tell you of the number eight.

Eight days are for a B'rit, Seven days make up a week, Six are the Mishnah's Orders, Five books of Moses, Four is the Matriarchs, Three is the Patriarchs, Two tables of the Law, One is almighty God, almighty God. ...

Who can tell me of the number nine? I can tell you of the number nine.

Nine months to childbirth, Eight days are for a B'rit, Seven days make up a week, Six are the Mishnah's Orders, Five books of Moses, Four is the Matriarchs, Three is the Patriarchs, Two tables of the Law, One is almighty God, almighty God. ...

Who can tell me of the number ten? I can tell you of the number ten.

Ten for the Commandments, Nine months to childbirth, Eight days are for a B'rit, Seven days make up a week, Six are the Mishnah's Orders, Five books of Moses, Four is the Matriarchs, Three is the Patriarchs, Two tables of the Law, One is almighty God, almighty God. ...

Who can tell me of the number eleven? I can tell you of the number eleven.

Eleven stars in Joseph's dream, Ten for the Commandments, Nine months to childbirth, Eight days are for a B'rit, Seven days make up a week, Six are the Mishnah's orders, Five books of Moses, Four is the Matriarchs, Three is the Patriarchs, Two tables of the Law, One is almighty God, almighty God. ...

Who can tell me of the number twelve? I can tell you of the number twelve.

Twelve tribes of Israel, Eleven stars in Joseph's dream, Ten for the Commandments, Nine months to childbirth, Eight days are for a B'rit, Seven days make up a week, Six are the Mishnah's Orders, Five books of Moses, Four is the Matriarchs, Three is the Patriarchs, Two tables of the Law, One is almighty God, almighty God. ...

Who can tell me of the number thirteen? I can tell you of the number thirteen.

Thirteen Attributes of God, Twelve tribes of Israel, Eleven stars in Joseph's dream, Ten for the Commandments, Nine months to childbirth, Eight days are for a B'rit, Seven days make up a week, Six are the Mishnah's Orders, Five books of Moses, Four is the Matriarchs, Three is the Patriarchs, Two tables of the Law, One is almighty God, almighty God. ...

קרב יום | KA-REIV YOM

קָרֵב יוֹם, קָרֵב יוֹם,
אֲשֶׁר הוּא לֹא יוֹם וְלֹא לַיְלָה.
רָם הוֹדַע, הוֹדַע, הוֹדַע,
כִּי לְךָ הַיּוֹם, אַף לְךָ הַלַּיְלָה.
שׁוֹמְרִים הַפְקֵד לְעִירְךָ,
כָּל־הַיּוֹם וְכָל־הַלַּיְלָה.
תָּאִיר כְּאוֹר יוֹם חֶשְׁכַת לַיְלָה.

Ka-reiv yom, ka-reiv yom
a-sher hu lo yom v'lo lai-la.
Ram ho-da ki l'cha ha-yom
af l'cha ha-lai-la.
Sho-m'rim haf-keid l'ir'cha
kol ha-yom v'chol ha-lai-la
Ta-ir k'or yom chesh-chat lai-la.

p. 99

Bring near the day that is neither day nor night.
Declare, Most High, that the day is Yours, and Yours the night.
Place sentries over Your City all the day and all the night.
Make bright as the light of day the darkness of night.

ANA HALACH DODEICH

אָנָה הָלַךְ דּוֹדֵךְ,
הַיָּפָה בַּנָּשִׁים?
אָנָה פָּנָה דוֹדֵךְ?
וּנְבַקְשֶׁנּוּ עִמָּךְ.
דּוֹדִי יָרַד לְגַנּוֹ, לַעֲרוּגוֹת
הַבֹּשֶׂם.

A-na ha-lach do-deich,
ha-yafa ba-nashim?
A-na pa-na do-deich?
U-n'vak-shei-nu i-mach.
Do-di ya-rad l'ga-no, la-aru-got
ha-bo-sem.

p. 100

Where has your love gone, O fairest of women?
Where has your love gone to? Let us help you seek him.
My love has gone to his garden, to the beds of spices.

DODI LI

דּוֹדִי לִי וַאֲנִי לוֹ הָרֹעֶה
בַּשׁוֹשַׁנִּים.
מִי זֹאת עֹלָה מִן־הַמִּדְבָּר,
מִי זֹאת עֹלָה?
מְקֻטֶּרֶת מוֹר וּלְבוֹנָה,
מוֹר וּלְבוֹנָה.
לִבַּבְתִּנִי אֲחֹתִי כַלָּה,
לִבַּבְתִּנִי כַלָּה.
עוּרִי צָפוֹן, וּבוֹאִי תֵימָן
עוּרִי צָפוֹן, וּבוֹאִי תֵימָן.

Do-di li va-a-ni lo,
ha-ro-eh ba-sho-sha-nim.
Mi zot o-lah min ha-mid-bar,
mi zot o-lah?
M'ku-teh-ret mor, mor u-l'vo-na,
mor u-l'vo-na.
Li-bav-ti-ni, a-cho-ti ka-la,
li-bav-ti-ni ka-la.
U-ri tza-fon, u-vo-i tei-man,
U-ri tza-fon, u-vo-i tei-man.

My beloved is mine, and I am his, who pastures among the lilies. Who is that coming out of the desert, who is it? Anointed with myrrh, myrrh and frankincense. You have taken my heart, my sister, my bride; you have taken my heart. Rise up, O North Wind, and come, O South wind.

EL GINAT EGOZ

אֶל־גִּנַּת אֱגוֹז יָרַדְתִּי,
לִרְאוֹת בְּאִבֵּי הַנָּחַל,
לִרְאוֹת הֲפָרְחָה הַגֶּפֶן,
הֵנֵצוּ הָרִמֹּנִים.
לְכָה דוֹדִי, נֵצֵא הַשָּׂדֶה,
נָלִינָה בַּכְּפָרִים,
נַשְׁכִּימָה לַכְּרָמִים,
נִרְאֶה אִם פָּרְחָה הַגֶּפֶן,
פִּתַּח הַסְּמָדַר.
עוּרִי צָפוֹן, וּבוֹאִי תֵימָן,
הָפִיחִי גַנִּי, יִזְּלוּ בְשָׂמָיו,
יָבֹא דוֹדִי לְגַנּוֹ, וְיֹאכַל
פְּרִי מְגָדָיו.

El gi-nat eh-goz ya-rad-ti li-r'ot
b'i-bei ha-na-chal, li-r'ot
ha-far'cha ha-geh-fen, hei-nei-tzu
ha-ri-mo-nim. L'cha do-di, nei-tzei
ha-sa-eh, na-li-na ba-k'fa-rim,
nash-ki-ma la-k'ra-mim nir-eh
im par'cha ha-geh-fen pi-tach
ha-s'ma-dar. U-ri tza-fon, u-vo-i
tei-man. hafichi gani, yizlu
v'samav yavo dodi l'gano
v'yochal p'ri m'gadav.

I went down to the grove to see the valley break into flower, to see if the vines had blossomed, if the pomegranates were in bloom. Come, my beloved, let us go into the field and lie down among the flowers. Let us go early to the vineyards; let us see if the vine has flowered, if its blossoms have opened. Awake, O north wind, come, O south wind! Blow upon my garden, that its perfume may spread. Let my beloved come to his garden and enjoy its luscious fruits!

LET MY PEOPLE GO

When Israel was in Egypt land,
Let my people go.
Oppressed so hard they could not stand.
Let my people go.
Go down Moses, way down in Egypt land,
Tell ol' Pharaoh, let my people go.

Thus saith the Lord, bold Moses said,
Let my people go.
If not I'll smite your firstborn dead,
Let my people go.

Go down Moses, way down in Egypt land,
Tell ol' Pharaoh, let my people go.

As Israel stood by the water side,
Let my people go.
By God's command it did divide,
Let my people go.

Go down Moses, way down in Egypt land,
Tell ol' Pharaoh, let my people go.

p. 100
p.101

AN ONLY KID

p. 101

חַד גַּדְיָא חַד גַּדְיָא,	Chad gadya, chad gadya,
דְּזַבִּן אַבָּא בִּתְרֵי זוּזֵי;	diz'van a-ba bit-rei zu-zei;
חַד גַּדְיָא, חַד גַּדְיָא.	chad gadya, chad gadya.
וְאָתָא שׁוּנְרָא וְאָכַל לְגַדְיָא,	V'ata shun-ra v'a-chal l'gadya,
דְּזַבִּן אַבָּא בִּתְרֵי זוּזֵי;	diz'van a-ba bit-rei zu-zei;
חַד גַּדְיָא, חַד גַּדְיָא.	chad gadya, chad gadya.
וְאָתָא כַלְבָּא וְנָשַׁךְ לְשׁוּנְרָא,	V'a-ta chal-ba v'na-shach l'shun-ra,
דְּאָכַל לְגַדְיָא	d'a-chal l'gadya,
דְּזַבִּן אַבָּא בִּתְרֵי זוּזֵי;	diz'van a-ba bit-rei zu-zei;
חַד גַּדְיָא, חַד גַּדְיָא.	chad gadya, chad gadya.
וְאָתָא חוּטְרָא וְהִכָּה לְכַלְבָּא,	V'a-ta chut-ra v'hi-ka l'chal-ba,
דְּנָשַׁךְ לְשׁוּנְרָא דְּאָכַל לְגַדְיָא,	d'na-shach l'shun-ra, d'a-chal l'gadya,
דְּזַבִּן אַבָּא בִּתְרֵי זוּזֵי;	diz'van a-ba bit-rei zu-zei;
חַד גַּדְיָא, חַד גַּדְיָא.	chad gadya, chad gadya.

וְאָתָא נוּרָא וְשָׂרַף לְחוּטְרָא,
דְּהִכָּה לְכַלְבָּא דְּנָשַׁךְ לְשׁוּנְרָא,
דְּאָכַל לְגַדְיָא,
דְּזַבִּן אַבָּא בִּתְרֵי זוּזֵי;
חַד גַּדְיָא, חַד גַּדְיָא.

V'a-ta nu-ra v'sa-raf l'chutra,
d'hi-ka l'chal-ba, d'na-shach l'shun-ra,
d'achal l'gadya,
diz'van a-ba bit-rei zu-zei;
chad gadya, chad gadya.

וְאָתָא מַיָּא וְכָבָה לְנוּרָא,
דְּשָׂרַף לְחוּטְרָא דְּהִכָּה לְכַלְבָּא,
דְּנָשַׁךְ לְשׁוּנְרָא דְּאָכַל לְגַדְיָא,
דְּזַבִּן אַבָּא בִּתְרֵי זוּזֵי;
חַד גַּדְיָא, חַד גַּדְיָא.

V'a-ta ma-ya v'ch-ava l'nu-ra,
d'saraf l'chu-tra, d'hi-ka l'chalba,
d'na-shach l'shun-ra, d'achal l'gadya,
diz'van a-ba bit-rei zu-zei;
chad gadya, chad gadya.

וְאָתָא תוֹרָא וְשָׁתָה לְמַיָּא,
דְּכָבָה לְנוּרָא דְּשָׂרַף לְחוּטְרָא,
דְּהִכָּה לְכַלְבָּא דְּנָשַׁךְ לְשׁוּנְרָא,
דְּאָכַל לְגַדְיָא,
דְּזַבִּן אַבָּא בִּתְרֵי זוּזֵי;
חַד גַּדְיָא, חַד גַּדְיָא.

V'a-ta to-ra v'sha-ta l'ma-ya,
d'cha-va l'nu-ra, d'sa-raf l'chut-ra,
d'hi-ka l'chal-ba, d'na-shach l'shun-ra,
d'a-chal l'gadya,
diz'van a-ba bit-rei zu-zei;
chad gadya, chad gadya.

וְאָתָא הַשּׁוֹחֵט וְשָׁחַט לְתוֹרָא,
דְּשָׁתָה לְמַיָּא דְּכָבָה לְנוּרָא,
דְּשָׂרַף לְחוּטְרָא דְּהִכָּה לְכַלְבָּא,
דְּנָשַׁךְ לְשׁוּנְרָא דְּאָכַל לְגַדְיָא,
דְּזַבִּן אַבָּא בִּתְרֵי זוּזֵי;
חַד גַּדְיָא, חַד גַּדְיָא.

V'a-ta ha-sho-chet v'sh-chat l'to-ra,
d'sha-ta l'ma-ya, d'cha-va l'nu-ra,
d'sa-raf l'chut-ra, d'hi-ka l'chal-ba,
d'na-shach l'shun-ra, d'a-chal l'gadya,
diz'van a-ba bit-rei zu-zei;
chad gadya, chad gadya.

וְאָתָא מַלְאַךְ הַמָּוֶת וְשָׁחַט לַשּׁוֹחֵט,
דְּשָׁחַט לְתוֹרָא דְּשָׁתָה לְמַיָּא,
דְּכָבָה לְנוּרָא דְּשָׂרַף לְחוּטְרָא,
דְּהִכָּה לְכַלְבָּא דְּנָשַׁךְ לְשׁוּנְרָא,
דְּאָכַל לְגַדְיָא,
דְּזַבִּן אַבָּא בִּתְרֵי זוּזֵי;
חַד גַּדְיָא, חַד גַּדְיָא.

V'a-ta mal-ach ha-ma-vet,
v'sha-chat la-sho-chet,
d'sha-chat l'to-ra, d'sha-ta l'ma-ya,
d'cha-va l'nu-ra, d'sa-raf l'chut-ra,
d'hi-ka l'chal-ba, d'na-shach l'shun-ra,
d'a-chal l'gadya,
diz'van a-ba bit-rei zu-zei;
chad gadya, chad gadya.

וְאָתָא הַקָּדוֹשׁ בָּרוּךְ הוּא,
וְשָׁחַט לְמַלְאַךְ הַמָּוֶת,
דְּשָׁחַט לַשּׁוֹחֵט דְּשָׁחַט לְתוֹרָא,
דְּשָׁתָה לְמַיָּא דְּכָבָה לְנוּרָא,
דְּשָׂרַף לְחוּטְרָא דְּהִכָּה לְכַלְבָּא,
דְּנָשַׁךְ לְשׁוּנְרָא דְּאָכַל לְגַדְיָא,
דְּזַבִּן אַבָּא בִּתְרֵי זוּזֵי;
חַד גַּדְיָא, חַד גַּדְיָא.

V'a-ta ha-kadosh baruch hu,
v'sha-chat l'mal-ach ha-ma-vet
d'sha-chat la-sho-chet, d'sha-chat l'to-ra,
d'sha-ta l'ma-ya, d'cha-va l'nu-ra,
d'sa-raf l'chutra, d'hi-ka l'chalba,
d'na-shach l'shu-nra, d'a-chal l'gadya,
diz'van a-ba bit-rei zu-zei;
chad gadya, chad gadya.

CHAD GADYA

Chad gadya, chad gadya,
that father bought for two zuzim;
chad gadya, chad gadya.

p. 101

Then came the cat and ate the kid
that father bought for two zuzim;
chad gadya, chad gadya.

Then came the dog and bit the cat
that ate the kid
that father bought for two zuzim;
chad gadya, chad gadya.

Then came the stick and beat the dog
that bit the cat that ate the kid
that father bought for two zuzim;
chad gadya, chad gadya.

Then came the fire and burnt the stick
that beat the dog that bit the cat
that ate the kid
that father bought for two zuzim;
chad gadya, chad gadya.

Then came the water and quenched the fire
that burnt the stick that beat the dog
that bit the cat that ate the kid
that father bought for two Zuzim;
chad gadya, chad gadya.

Then came the ox and drank the water
that quenched the fire that burnt the stick
that beat the dog that bit the cat
that ate the kid
that father bought for two Zuzim;
chad gadya, chad gadya.

Then came the butcher and slew the ox
that drank the water that quenched the fire
that burnt the stick that beat the dog
that bit the cat that ate the kid
that father bought for two Zuzim;
chad gadya, chad gadya.

Along came the angel of death
and slew the butcher that slew the ox
that drank the water that quenched the fire
that burnt the stick that beat the dog
that bit the cat that ate the kid
that father bought for two Zuzim;
chad gadya, chad gadya.

Along came the Holy One,
the One who is blessed,
and slew the angel of death
that slew the butcher
that slew the ox
that drank the water
that quenched the fire
that burnt the stick
that beat the dog
that bit the cat
that ate the kid
that father bought for two Zuzim;
chad gadya, chad gadya.

Candle Lighting

A. W. Binder

Kiddush

Trad. Arr. by Kenneth B. Cohen

man chei-ru-tei-nu, (b' a-ha-va) mik-ra ko - desh, zei-cher li-tsi-at Mits-ra - yim. Ki

va - - nu va-char - - ta v'o-ta - - nu li -

dash - - - ta mi - kol ha-a-mim, (v'shab-bat) u' mo-a-dei_ lod-sh' cha_ (b'

a-ha-va uv' ra-tson,)b'sim-cha uv' sa-son_ hin-chal-ta - - - nu. Bu-

ruch a-ta A-do-nai m' ka-deish (Ha-shab-bat v')Yis-ra - el
Yis-ra - el v' haz'ma-nim

ruch a-ta A-do-nai, E - lo - hei - nu me-lech ha-o - lam, she - he - che - ya - nu, v'

ki -y' ma - nu, v' hi - gi - ya - nu laz' - - - man ha - - zeh.

Ha Lachma

Learned from Pinchas Stern

Recited freely

Ha _ lach-ma an-ya di a - cha-lu a-va-ha-ta-na b' ar' a d'mitz - ra - yim.

kol dich-fin yei-tei v' yei - chul, _
kol dits-rich yei-tei v' yif - sach. _
Ha-sha-ta ha-cha,_ la-sha-na ha-ba'

a, b' ar'a d'yis-ra' el. Ha-sha-ta av-dei, la-sha-na ha-ba' a _ b' nei cho-rin._

Ma Nishtana

Inquisitively   Israeli

Ma nish-ta-na ha - lai - la ha-zeh mi - kol___ ha - lei -
chol ha-lai-lot   a - nu och-lin cha - meitz___ u - ma -

lot?   mi - kol___ ha - lei - lot?   She-b'
tza,   cha - meitz___   u - ma -   tza,   ha -

lai - la ha-zeh   ha - lai - la ha-zeh   ku - lo___ ma - -

tzah ___ ha - tzah.   *Fine*   She-b'   *D.C. al Fine*

Ma Nishtana

Recited freely   *Lern-Steiger* (Study Mode)

Ma   nish-ta-na ha-lai-la ha - zeh___   mi - kol   ha-lei - lot? ___

Verses

She - b' chol   ha - lei - lot a - nu och - lin cha - meitz   u - ma -

tzah, ___   ha - lai - la ha - zeh___   ku - lo___ ma - tzah. ___

Dayeinu

Lively   Israeli

1. I - lu   I - lu   ho - tsi a - nu,   ho - tsi - a - nu   mi - mits-ra - yim,
2. I - lu na - tan   na - tan la - nu,   na - tan - la - nu   et ha - shab - bat,
3. I - lu na - tan   na - tan la - nu,   na - tan - la - nu   et ha - to - rah,

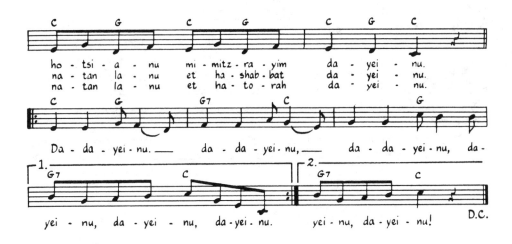

ho - tsi - a - nu mi - mitz - ra - yim da - yei - nu.
na - tan la - nu et ha - shab - bat da - yei - nu.
na - tan la - nu et ha - to - rah da - yei - nu.

Da - da - yei - nu.___ da - da - yei - nu,___ da - da - yei - nu, da -

1. yei - nu, da - yei - nu, da - yei - nu. **2.** yei - nu, da - yei - nu!

D.C.

B'tzeit Yisrael

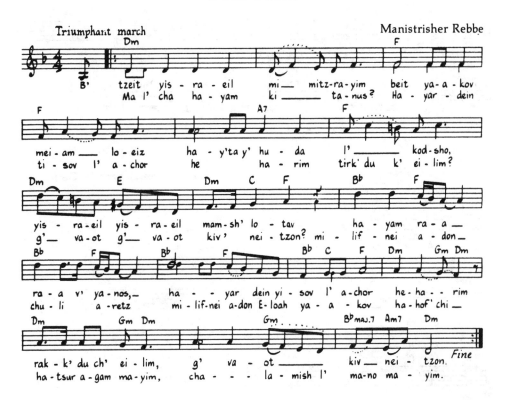

Triumphant march

Manistrisher Rebbe

B' tzeit yis - ra - eil mi - mitz - ra - yim beit ya - a - kov
Ma l' cha ha - yam ki ___ ta - nus? Ha - yar - dein

mei - am ___ lo - eiz ha - y'ta y' hu - da l' ___ kod - sho,
ti - sov l' a - chor he ha - rim tirk' du k' ei - lim?

yis - ra - eil yis - ra - eil mam - sh' lo - tav ha - yam ra - a ___
g' - va - ot g' - va - ot kiv' nei - tzon? mi - lif - nei a - don ___

ra - a v' ya - nos, ___ ha - - yar dein yi - sov l' a - chor he - ha - - rim
chu - li a - retz mi - lif - nei a - don E - loah ya - a - kov ha - hof' chi ___

rak - k' du ch' ei - lim, g' va - ot ___ kiv ___ nei - tzon.
ha - tsur a - gam ma - yim, cha - - la - mish l' ma - no ma - yim.

Fine

Eliyahu Hanavi

Softly with longing

Folk Song

Ei - li - ya - hu ha - na - vi, Ei - li - ya - hu ha - tish - bi,

Ei - li - ya - hu Ei - li - ya - hu Ei - li - ya - hu ha - gil - a - di.

Fine

With optimism

bim - hei - ra b' ya - mei - nu ya - vo ei - lei - nu

Im - ma - shi - ach ben Da - vid Im - ma - shi - ach ben Da - vid.

D.C. al Fine

Ki Lo Na-eh

With reverence

With a lilt   M. Nathanson

Ki lo na - eh ki lo ya - eh.

1. A - dir bim - lu - cha,
2. Da - gul bim - lu - cha,

March

ba - chur ka - ha - la - chah, ge - du - dav yom' ru lo, le - cha u' le - cha le -

ha - dar ka - ha - la - chah, va - ti - kav yom' ru lo, le -

cha ki le - cha le - cha af le - cha, le - cha A - do - nai ha - mam - la - cha.

D.C.

Adir Hu

Majestically

J. S. Rittangels Haggadah – Germany

Repeat this bar as needed
in remaining verses.

1. A - dir hu, a - dir hu, yig - a - lei - nu b' ka - rov,
2. Awe - some One, awe - some One, soon may You re - deem us,
3. God of might, God of right, Rock of our sal - va - tion,

bim - hei - ra ____ bim - hei - ra b' ya - mei - nu b' ka - - rov.

speed - i - ly, ____ speed - i - ly, ____ soon with - in our life - time.

un - to You ____ still we do ____ of - fer A - dor - a - tion.

Eil p' dei, Eil p' dei, p' dei am' cha b' ka - rov

Save, O God; Save, O God, ____ Save Your peo - ple speed - i - ly.

Since Your hand from E - gypt's land ____ led Your joy - ful Na - tion.

D.C.

Echad Mi Yodea

Gaily

Israeli

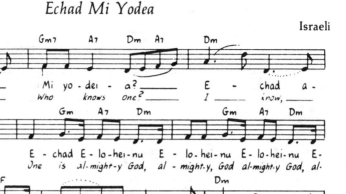

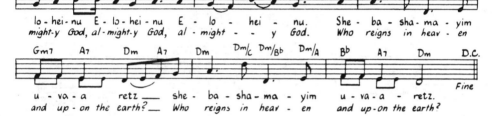

VERSES: E - chad Mi yo-dei - a? _____ E - chad a-
Who _____ knows, _____ Who knows one? _____ I know, _____

ni yo-dei - a E-chad E-lo-hei-nu E - lo-hei-nu E - lo-hei-nu E-
I know one. One is al-might-y God, al - might-y, God al-might-y God, al-

lo-hei-nu E - lo-hei-nu E - lo - hei - nu. She - ba-sha-ma - yim
might-y God, al-might-y God, al - might - - y God. Who reigns in heav - en

u - va - a - retz _____ she - ba-sha-ma - yim u-va-a - retz.
and up-on the earth? _____ Who reigns in heav - en and up-on the earth?

Echad Mi Yodea

Joyously

Oriental Community in Jerusalem

VERSES: E - chad _____ mi yo-dei - a? E-chad _____ a-ni yo-dei - a E-

chad E - lo - hei - - nu sheh ba-sha-ma - yim _____ u-va-a - rets.

Kareiv Yom

Mysteriously

Chassidic Folk Song

Ka - reiv yom ka - reiv _____ yom _____ a - sher hu - lo yom v' lo-lai - la.

Ram _____ ho-da ho-da ho-da ki l' cha-ha yom _____ af l' cha ha-lai - la.

Shom' rim haf-keid haf-keid l' ir - cha _____ kol ha-yom _____ v' chol ha - lai - la.
Ta - ir k' or k' or _____ yom chesh - chat _____ yom _____ lai - la.

Ana Halach Dodeich

Let My People Go!

Let My People Go!

Chad Gadya

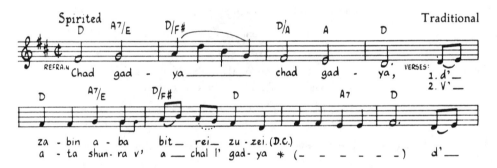

*After each new verse, repeat prior verses, then D.C.

Much of the music of the Seder comes from ancient and medieval sources. Throughout our history, Jewish composers have returned to cantillation as the earliest source of our musical tradition. A. W. Binder contends that biblical cantillation is the basis of our prayer modes, traditional melodies (i.e., *Kol Nidre*), folk songs, and art music. Biblical cantillation inspires us even today (see, e.g., *Ana Halach Dodeich*, based on the Ashkenazic cantillation for *Shir Hashirim*—Song of Songs). Examples of later influences upon the music of the Seder are found in the *Kiddush* (Germany, 11th–13th centuries) and *Adir Hu* (Germany, 17th century).

In every generation and locale, Jews have sought to relive the Exodus through the words of the Seder and through its music. For this music we have looked to the past, and have, in age after age, created new expressions to celebrate the miracle of freedom. May Israel's song ever be acceptable to God, who created us to be free.

Notes

Abbreviations and Notations

Abrahams	Israel Abrahams, *A Companion to the Authorized Daily Prayerbook* (page references to Hermon Press edition, New York, 1966).
AMPH	*A Modern Passover Haggadah*, edited by John D. Rayner in collaboration with Chaim Stern and with the assistance of Rabbi Julia Neuberger, under the aegis of: the Rabbinic Conference of the Union of Liberal and Progressive Synagogues (ULPS), (ULPS, London, 1981).
CS	Rabbi Chaim Stern (editor of this Haggadah; and see AMPH)
EJ	*Encyclopaedia Judaica* (Keter Publishing House, Ltd., Jerusalem, 1972)
Goldschmidt	E. D. Goldschmidt, *Haggadah shel Pesach V'toldoteha* (Bialik Institute, Jerusalem, 1969)
JDR	Rabbi John D. Rayner (principal editor of AMPH).
JE	*Jewish Encyclopedia* (Funk & Wagnalls Company, New York and London, 1907)
Kasher	Menachem M. Kasher, *Haggadah Shelemah* (Torah Shelemah Institute, Jerusalem, 1967)
Mishnah	Fundamental Rabbinic law-compilation completed in Palestine in the third century C.E.
MODERN	A passage appearing in a previous modern Haggadah, but not in the traditional Haggadah.
NEW	A passage newly written for the present Haggadah. It may also appear in AMPH, sometimes with changes.
NOVEL	A passage first utilized (so far as we know) in the present Haggadah. It may also appear in AMPH. Such a passage may be Biblical, Rabbinic, or contemporary.
NUH	*The New Union Haggadah*, edited by Rabbi Herbert Bronstein for the Central Conference of American Rabbis (CCAR, New York, 1974)
O.Ch.	*Orach Chayim* (Part I of the Arba-ah Turim, the fourteenth century law-code by Jacob ben Asher of Germany and Spain; likewise of the Shulchan Aruch, the sixteenth century law-code by Joseph Caro of Palestine with glosses by Moses Isserles of Poland)
R.	Rabbi
SPJH	*Services and Prayers for Jewish Homes*, the prayerbook of the Liberal Jewish Synagogue (London) published in 1918. It contained the first British Liberal Haggadah. It was revised in 1955 and published by the ULPS. The ULPS published an entirely new Haggadah, edited by JDR, 1962, now replaced by AMPH.
SRA	*Seder Rav Amram*, the first Jewish prayerbook, compiled by Amram ben Sheshna, Gaon of Sura, Babylonia, about 860 C.E. (page references to E. D. Goldschmidt's edition, Mossad Harav Kook, Jerusalem, 1971)
Talmud	Refers either to the Babylonian Talmud, completed approximately in the sixth century C.E., or the Jerusalem (also called Palestinian) Talmud, completed in the fourth century C.E.
Tosafot	Super-commentaries on the Babylonian Talmud by Franco-German scholars of the twelfth and thirteenth centuries.
TRAD.	A passage appearing in the traditional Haggadah.
ULPS	Union of Liberal and Progressive Synagogues (London)

A General Note on Translation

PAGE xiii, (and often elsewhere): The traditional benediction-formula (Baruch ata Adonai, Eloheinu melech haolam…) has always been a problem to translate. Our translation is: "We praise You, Eternal One…," but the reader is reminded that translations are many and varied. We shall here discuss two of the six Hebrew words that introduce the formula: *Baruch* and *Adonai*. We have left the second half of the formula untranslated.

The word "Baruch" is a passive participle meaning "blessed" or "praised." So translated it leads to awkward English, such as "Praised are You." One attempt to solve the problem is to treat the second word (*ata*, "You") as though it weren't there, so that we get "Blessed is…" We have chosen instead to mistranslate the Hebrew so as to produce a simple English declaration, "We praise…" recognizing that the verb is now active rather than passive, but feeling that it is the least bad Englishing of an elusive Hebrew locution.

The word "Adonai" is equally interesting. Usually it is translated as "Lord." It is an accurate translation for the word that, long ago, was introduced as a *substitute* for the pronouncing of the sacred Name of God, which is spelled (unvocalized) YHVH but pronounced ADONAI, from ADON, "LORD." "Lord" has the virtue, also, of being a word with four letters, and it is in that respect reminiscent of the four-letter Divine Name YHVH. There are, however, two objections that may be laid against the use of "Lord" for YHVH: it is masculine, and God has no gender and should not be spoken of in exclusively masculine terms; and it fails to convey to the English reader the root-meaning of YHVH, which is related to the verb for *being*. God (YHVH, Adonai) is the One-Who-Is-Was-Will Be. Therefore, we have chosen to render Adonai (and in this we follow, among others, the German usage) by "Eternal," or "Eternal One."

The benediction-formula we have been discussing has two forms, "long" and "short." Both appear in the Haggadah. The long form contains the words "asher kid'shanu b'mitzvotav," rendered by some as "who has sanctified (or, hallowed) us with His commandments." We prefer simply to allude to the Mitzvah, a word that does not require translation.

PAGE 17 (The Four Questions): The opening sentence is in fact an exclamation: "How different is this night from all other nights!" Because the less accurate "Why is this night different…" is so well-known and preferred, we have chosen to retain it.

PAGE 18 (The Four Children): The "children" are often called the "four sons." We have preferred to be more general, knowing that there are as many daughters as sons. Similarly, the introductory Hebrew is in the masculine singular; our English is plural: "The questions children ask." We believe we are being faithful to the intent of the Hebrew. It should be borne in mind that the Seder is a group ceremony, and the use of the plural, where the English is likely to be read, serves to include all the celebrants, and that is all to the good. This comment applies as well, and perhaps especially, to the passage on page 31 ("Arami oveid avi") literally, "My father was a wandering Aramean." In its original setting (Deuteronomy 26) it was a formula to be recited by *individuals* in a thanksgiving ceremony; here, in the Seder, its function is communal, and it seems right, therefore, to translate it into the plural.

In general, it seems to us that the occasional translation of Hebrew singulars as English plurals, and of third person to second, has a beneficial effect. Thus, for example, page 35: "You Yourself… in all Your glory" gains power from its direct address, and is to be preferred over the literal "He Himself . . . in all His glory."

This Note would not be complete without this demurrer: the foregoing should not mislead the reader into supposing that the Hebrew has not been faithfully translated. Almost always, it has not been necessary to make changes; and the few changes noted above are a faithful, if not always a literal, movement from Hebrew, a Semitic language, into English, very much non-Semitic in nature; and from texts written two or three thousand years ago into English that must mediate between past and present. No translation is the original. This translation proposes to reproduce the emotional reality behind the Hebrew. If we have caught something of its ethos, we are content.

Sources

Page

3   *Long ago…* NEW, by JDR and CS. Based in part on a new prayer by CS in *Gates of Prayer* (CCAR, New York, 1975), p.460.

4   *The people who walked in darkness…* NOVEL, Isaiah. 9:1. The following sentence ("From bondage") is NEW, by CS.

4   *We praise… Yom Tov.* The custom of kindling lights to inaugurate the Sabbath or a Festival is taken for granted in the (second century) Mishnah (Shabbat 2:6) and in the Talmud (B. Pesachim 102b), but the benediction is first found in post-talmudic sources (SRA, p. 61; Shulchan Aruch, O.Ch. 263:5, 514:11). The Chanukah benediction is exceptional, being found already in the Talmud, B. Shabbat 23a.

4   *Light is the great…* NEW, by CS.

5   *For all of us…* NEW, by CS.

5   *May God bless you…* TRAD., Numbers 6:24f. The custom of parents blessing their children on the eve of a Sabbath or a Festival is first mentioned in early seventeenth century sources (JE, III, p. 243; EJ, 4, p. 1097). The concept of parental blessing in general plays an important part already in the Bible (e.g., Genesis 27 and 48f.), and Soferim 18:5 mentions a custom of bringing thirteen-year-old boys to be blessed by the elders in Jerusalem.

6   *Tonight we drink…* NOVEL. "Not less than four cups of wine are ordained already in the Mishnah (Pesachim 10:1). "Four corners of the earth and "Four seasons of the year": Midrash Agur 5:100. "Four world empires": Jerusalem (Palestinian) Talmud Pesachim 10:1; "Four promises of redemption": *ibid.* and Genesis Rabbah 88:5. On these and other explanations for the drinking of four cups at the Seder, see Kasher, pp. 90-94.

6   *We will drink…* NEW, by CS.

7   *I am the Eternal…* MODERN, Exodus 6:6. The idea of reciting before each cup the appropriate clause from Exodus 6:6f. is found already in NUH. More generally, many modern Haggadot have introductions to the cups; their themes vary.

8   *We praise… vine.* TRAD. The benediction to be said before drinking wine as ordained in the Mishnah (Berachot 6:1; Pesachim 10:2).

8   *Eternal God…Israel.* TRAD. Known as *Kiddush,* short for *Kiddush Hayom,* Sanctification of the Day, this benediction is often referred to in Rabbinic Literature (Mishnah Pesachim 10:2; Babylonian Talmud: Pesachim l05a, Beitzah 17a), but the full text is first found in post-talmudic sources (Soferim 19:2; SRA, pp. 110f.)

9   *We praise… fire.* TRAD., Mishnah Berachot 8:5. When the Sabbath is followed by a Festival, the custom is not to light a special candle as when it is followed by an ordinary day, but merely to look at the already-kindled Festival lights when reciting this benediction (which is cited in Mishnah Berachot 8:5).

9   *We praise… O God.* TRAD., the principal benediction *of the Havdalah* ("Separation" or "Distinction") ceremony according to the version used when the Sabbath is followed by a Festival. It is first cited in the Babylonian Talmud: Pesachim 103b.

9   *We praise… this season.* Known as *Shehecheyanu,* this is the benediction recited at the beginning of a Festival (and on other happy occasions). It is cited in various places in the Babylonian Talmud, including Pesachim 7b.

10   *Spring hangs...* The opening sentence, in quotation marks, is from a poem, *Tirocinium*, by William Cowper. The rest of the passage is adapted from a NEW passage by JDR in AMPH.

10   *Rise up, my love...* MODERN, Songs of Songs 2:11f. Traditionally, the Song of Songs is read on the morning of the Sabbath in Pesach, though at one time it was read on the last two eves (see Soferim 14:18). There is also a custom to read it after the Seder; hence it is found at the end of some Haggadot. The quotation from it in the present context was an innovation of SPJH, and it is found in many modern Haggadot. The second stanza ("The standing corn...") is from *Tal*, the prayer for "Dew," traditionally inserted in the *Musaf* (Additional) service on the first day of Pesach. The present passage is an excerpt from a version of Tal that appears in the *Sephardi* liturgy. The translation, by CS, appeared first in GOP, p. 493, where it serves as an introductory prayer in the Pesach morning service. Its use here is an innovation of this Haggadah.

10   *The green herbs are dipped in salt water...* TRAD. The Mishnah (Pesachim 10:3) says that *Chazeret*, lettuce, is to be dipped, but does not make it clear in what. The custom of using *Karpas*, parsley, and of dipping it in salt water (or vinegar), symbolic of the tears shed by the Israelite slaves in Egypt (and, secondarily, of the ocean in which life was born), is first mentioned in Medieval sources (Tosafot to Babylonian Talmud, Pesachim 114a; Shulchan Aruch, O.Ch. 473:4; see Kasher, pp.101-106).

10   *We praise... earth.* TRAD. The benediction to be recited, according to the Mishnah (Berachot 6:1), before eating any fruit or vegetable grown on the ground.

11   *One of the company takes out...* The plain reason for the three Matzot is that the top and bottom ones correspond to the two loaves of bread customary on the eve of the Sabbath or a Festival (in allusion, it is said, to the double portion of Manna granted the Israelites for the Sabbath in their wandering through the wilderness, Exodus 16:22), while the middle one represents the "bread of affliction" (Deuteronomy 16:3). Medieval sources also give fanciful explanations, e.g., that the three Matzot refer to the Three Patriarchs (Abraham, Isaac, and Jacob), or the three measures of flour with which Sarah baked bread for the three angelic visitors (Genesis 18:6), or the three classes of Israelites (Priest, Levite, Israelite) into which the people were divided in ancient times. See Kasher, pp. 61f.

11   *This is the bread of affliction...* TRAD. An Aramaic formula first found, in various forms, in Gaonic Rites (see SRA, p.113; Kasher, pp. 106-112; Goldschmidt, pp. 7f.). The first sentence alludes to Deuteronomy 16:3; the second is based on an invitation to the poor to share one's meal found already in the Babylonian Talmud, Ta'anit 20b.

11   *As we eat...* NEW, by CS.

12   *Rabbi Bunam said...* NOVEL, from Chasidic literature.

12   *There are people...* NOVEL. A saying of Mohandas K. Gandhi.

13   *Rabban Gamaliel...* TRAD., already in the Mishnah, Pesachim 10:5. The reference is to Rabban Gamaliel I, grandson of Hillel. Gamaliel was Patriarch of Palestinian Jewry before the destruction of the Temple by the Romans in 70 C.E.

13   *Pesach: Why did our ancestors eat...* TRAD. Alluded to in the Mishnah, Pesachim 10:5. The full text is first found in SRA, p. 115, quoting Exodus 12:27.

13   *When the Temple still stood...* NEW, by CS and JDR. Also in AMPH, in slightly different form.

14   *This egg...* NEW, by JDR and CS Also in AMPH.

14   *Matzah: Why do we eat it...* TRAD. Alluded to in the Mishnah, Pesachim 10:5. The full text is first found in SRA, p. 115, quoting Exodus 12:39.

14 *Free Romans...* NEW, by CS and JDR. Also in AMPH, in rather different form, by JDR and CS. The custom of "leaning" or "reclining" is mentioned already in the Mishnah, Pesachim 10:1. The Jerusalem (Palestinian) Talmud comments: "To show that they had come forth from slavery to freedom" (Pesachim 10:1). Medieval sources record various opinions on this custom, discussing who should lean, and whether to lean at all (Shulchan Aruch, O.Ch. 472:2-7; Kasher, pp. 68-76).

15 *We praise... from the earth.* TRAD., the benediction to be recited before eating bread, as ordained in the Mishnah, Berachot 6:1. It alludes to Psalm 104:14.

15 *We praise... unleavened bread.* TRAD., first found, in a slightly different version, in SRA, p. 117.

15 *Maror: Why do we eat it...* TRAD. Alluded to in the Mishnah, Pesachim 10:5. First found in full in SRA, p. 115, quoting Exodus 1:14.

16 *Before eating the Maror...* NEW, by JDR, in AMPH. Here adapted by CS. Further on the Charoset, see Shulchan Aruch, O.Ch. 473:5 and Kasher, pp. 62-64.

16 *We praise... bitter herbs.* TRAD., first found, with slightly different wording, in SRA, p. 116.

16 *This was Hillel's practice...* TRAD., quoting Numbers 9:11. The Tosefta (Pesachim 2:14) and Babylonian Talmud (Pesachim 115a) allude to it; the Gaonic and subsequent Rites have the full text in various versions (see SRA, p. 117; Kasher, pp. 169f.). Hillel was the leading Pharisaic teacher in Palestine in the last decades of the first century B.C.E.

16 *We hold...* NEW, by CS.

17 *Why is this night different...* TRAD. First found in the Mishnah (Pesachim 10:4), but with *three* and somewhat different questions. By Gaonic times there was substantial modification and by SRA, p. 113, we have the text as now. See Kasher, pp. 112~117; Goldschmidt, pp. 10-13.

17 *You are free...* NEW, by CS.

18 *The questions children ask...* NOVEL, from the Mechilta d'Rabbi Shimon ben Yochai to Exodus 13:14. Also in AMPH.

18 *And parents should...* NOVEL, from the Mishnah, Pesachim 10:4. Also in AMPH.

18 *The Torah speaks...* TRAD. First found, in divergent versions, in Rabbinic Literature (Mechilta to Exodus 13:14 and the Jerusalem (Palestinian) Talmud, Pesachim 10:4) and, further modified, in the Gaonic Rites (See SRA, p. 114; Kasher, pp. 120-123; Goldschmidt, pp. 22-29). The wise child is derived from Deuteronomy 6:20 and Mishnah Pesachim 10:8; the wicked child from Exodus 12:26 and 13:8; the simple one from Exodus 13:14; and the one who does not know enough to ask from Exodus 13:8.

18 *You cannot be redeemed...* NOVEL, from Chasidic literature.

19 *Even in the lowliest...* NOVEL, from Chasidic literature, adapted by CS.

19 *The Koretzer...* NOVEL, from Chasidic literature.

19 *Hillel said...* NOVEL, from Pirké Avot 2:4b.

20 *He used to say...* NOVEL, from Pirké Avot 1:14. Another of Hillel's dicta.

20 *Will you seek...* NOVEL, by Walt Whitman, from *Leaves of Grass*.

20 *Every one of us...* NEW, by CS.

20 *On the side...* NOVEL, by Edmond Jabès.

21 *Our story begins...* NOVEL, from Mishnah Pesachim 10:4. Also in AMPH.

21   *We were slaves…* TRAD., mentioned in the Babylonian Talmud, Pesachim 116a, which says that the third century teacher Samuel advocated the recitation of this passage as fulfilling the principle to "begin with degradation and end with glory" (see preceding Note). The full text is first found in Gaonic Rites (See SRA, pp. 113f.; Kasher, pp. 117-120).

21   *Questions call…* NEW, by CS.

21   *If you think…* NOVEL, from Chasidic literature, adapted by CS.

22   *How are we to tell…* NEW, by CS, a comment on the passage that follows.

22   *They say…* TRAD. This Midrash is first found in Gaonic Rites (See SRA, p.114). The five rabbis mentioned lived in Palestine in the first-second centuries. B'nei B'rak was a place near Jaffa. It has been conjectured that the event described here took place just before the Bar Kochba revolt against Roman rule (132-135 C.E.), and that the rabbis were actually planning the revolt. That may or may not be. The Tosefta, a source parallel to the Mishnah, contains a similar story (See Tosefta, Pesachim 10.12), but with other characters, and taking place in Lydda, not B'nei B'rak.

22   *I can feel…* NOVEL, by Anne Frank, from her *Diary*.

23   *Rabbi Elazar ben Azariah…* TRAD., from Mishnah Berachot 1:5. Our translation is not literal.

23   *And then all…* NOVEL, by Judy Chicago.

24   *Our story begins…* TRAD. First mentioned in the Babylonian Talmud, Pesachim 116a, as the passage favored by the third century teacher Rav as fulfilling the principle to "begin with degradation and end with glory," as against his colleague Samuel, who favored the passage "We were slaves" (See above, last Note but three). The full text is first found in Gaonic Rites (See SRA, p.114; Kasher, pp. 27f.). The quotation is Joshua 24:2f.

24   *Our story begins…* NOVEL, from Mishnah Pesachim 10:4. Also in AMPH.

25   *Our ancestors…* TRAD., Deuteronomy 26:5-8. Mentioned already in the Mishnah, Pesachim 10:4, as the basis of the exposition which forms the bulk of the Haggadah-narrative. The translation here, as occasionally elsewhere in this Haggadah, departs from the literal in order to avoid liturgically unnecessary masculine language. The Hebrew is written in the singular ("My father was a wandering Aramean…."), meaning "forefather," and referring to Abraham, Jacob, or the Patriarchs collectively. The Editor prefers "ancestors," so that our "foremothers" may be included by us in our collective memory.

25   *There is an enslavement…* NEW, by CS.

26   *We began as wanderers…* NEW, by CS. Also in AMPH.

26   *Though upon our arrival…* NEW, by CS, alluding to Exodus 6:9. Also (with slight differences) in AMPH.

26   *The real slavery…* NOVEL. A saying of Rabbi Hanokh of Aleksandrow (1798-1870, Poland), quoted by Martin Buber in *Tales of the Hasidim*, Vol. 2, p. 315. Also in AMPH.

26   *Liberty is not less…* NOVEL, by Lucretia Mott.

26   *My very chains…* NOVEL, by George Gordon, Lord Byron, *The Prisoner of Chillon*, XIV. Also in AMPH.

27   *Our ancestors…* TRAD., Deuteronomy 10:22. First found in SRA, p.114. This translation renders a second person singular into first person plural.

27   *The use of the word…* TRAD.

27   *Jewish resistance…* NOVEL. A responsum by Rabbi Ephraim Oshry to a question asked by a fellow-concentration camp inmate, in *She-eilot U-t'shuvot Mima'amakim* ("Questions and Answers from the Depths").

28   *Two women…* NOVEL, two passages from the Midrash, Exodus Rabbah 1:14, 1:15, quoting Exodus 1:17.

28   *How did Israel…* NOVEL, from the Babylonian Talmud, Yevamot 79a.

28   *The people…* TRAD., Exodus 1:17. First found in SRA, p.114.

29   *As it is said…* TRAD., Exodus 1:8-10. First found in SRA, p. 114.

29   *Covey at length…* NOVEL, by Frederick Douglass.

30   *As it is said… Raamses.* TRAD., Exodus 1:11. First found in SRA, p. 114.

30   *As it is said… themselves.* TRAD., Exodus 1:13. First found in SRA, p. 114. The remainder of the passage is NOVEL, from the Midrash, Exodus Rabbah 5:18.

31   *As it is said… God.* TRAD., Exodus 2:23. First found in SRA, p.114.

31   *As it is said… covenant.* TRAD., Exodus 2:24. First found in SRA, p.114.

31   *And that covenant…* NEW, by CS.

31   *We have learned…* NOVEL, from the Midrash.

32   *It is said… God knew.* TRAD., Exodus 2:25.

32   *God saw… wives.* TRAD. First found in SRA, p. 114. It is based on a legend found in the Babylonian Talmud (Sotah 74b) that the Egyptians forbade the Israelites to procreate. The preceding passage (Exodus 2:25) is the prooftext for this observation, though the connection between them is not clear.

32   *It was said… Nile.* TRAD., Exodus 1:22. First found in SRA, p. 114. This becomes the prooftext for the next passage.

32   *God saw… children.* TRAD. First found in SRA, p. 114. In the traditional Haggadah, this passage *precedes* the previous one.

32   *And it is said… oppress them.* NOVEL, Exodus 3:9. Also in AMPH.

32   *The basic freedom…* NOVEL, by Margaret Sanger.

33   *God saw… our spirit.* NEW, by CS.

33   *God said: "How well I see"…* NOVEL, Exodus 3:7. Also in AMPH.

33   *I sit on a man's back…* NOVEL, by Leo Tolstoi.

33   *Even if you are a slave…* NOVEL, from a passage by John Ruskin, in *Fors Clavigera*, letter 46.

34   *Our plight…* NEW, by CS, introducing two NOVEL passages (both of which are also in AMPH): Judges 10:16 (here slightly adapted) and Isaiah 63:9, 21.

34   *And we have learned…* NOVEL, from the Babylonian Talmud, Megillah 29a. Also in AMPH.

34   *The less fit…* NOVEL, by John Stuart Mill, in *Subjugation of Women*, II:30.

35   *Not by an angel…* TRAD. First found in SRA, p.114, but based on a passage in the Jerusalem (Palestinian) Talmud, Sanhedrin 2:1 and Horayot 3:1.

35   *The Divine Presence…* TRAD. First found in SRA, p.114, quoting Deuteronomy 4:34.

36   *Our ancestors…* Part of the passage from Deuteronomy 25 that appears in full on p.25.

36   *Now let us call…* NEW, by CS.

36   *Then God led us…* A continuation of the passage from Deuteronomy referred to in the last note but one.

36   *We remember… carried off.* NEW, by CS.

37   *By the rivers...* NOVEL, Psalm 137:1-3.

37   *Break into songs...* NOVEL, Isaiah 52:9.

37   *When Greek invaders...* NEW, by CS.

37   *So it happened...* NOVEL, from II Maccabees 10.

37   *When Roman power... began to grow.* NEW, by CS.

38   *Once, as Rabban Yochanan...* NOVEL, from Avot d'Rabbi Natan, quoting Hosea 6:6.

38   *This Torah...* NEW, by CS.

38   *My word is like fire...* NOVEL, from Midrash Tanchuma, Noah § 3; Babylonian Talmud Sanhedrin 34a.

38   *We went forth... in hope.* NEW, by CS.

38   *O Zion...* NOVEL, by Judah Halevi. It is one of his "Zion" poems.

39   *The long nightmare...* NEW, by CS.

39   *I thought...* NOVEL, by Ephraim of Regensburg. A testimony from the Middle Ages.

39   *Now we call... Palestine.* NEW, by CS.

39   *I have not sung...* NOVEL, by Rachel Bluestein. Translated from the Hebrew by CS.

39   *We came... tyrants.* NEW, by CS.

40   *Your glory...* NOVEL, II Samuel 1:19, 23, 25.

40   *But we have outlived... free.* NEW, by CS.

40   *How beautiful...* NOVEL, Isaiah 52:7-8, 10.

41   *No liberation is easy...* NEW, by JDR and CS. Also (with some minor differences) in AMPH.

41   *Apathy in the face of evil...* NEW, by CS. An acrostic, with the first ten letters of the English alphabet, of evils, ancient and modern, to introduce the Ten Plagues.

41   *We look back now...* NEW, by CS.

41   *A drop of wine...* TRAD. The custom is mentioned in Medieval sources (see Shulchan Aruch, O.Ch., gloss; Kasher, p. 12f.). Our interpretation of it is based on that of Don Isaac Abravanel (1437-1508), who related it to the injunction, "Do not rejoice when your enemy falls," (Proverbs 24:17). For the Ten Plagues, see Exodus 7:14-12:36.

42   *When the cup of suffering...* NEW, by CS. Also in AMPH.

42   *At that time, when Israel stood...* NOVEL, from the Midrash, Mechilta to Exodus 14:22. Nachshon was a chieftain of the tribe of Judah; see Numbers 2:3, 10:14. Also in AMPH.

43   *At that time, they plunged...* NOVEL, from the Midrash, Exodus Rabbah 21:10. Also in AMPH, in abridged form.

43   *The people overcame...* NEW, by CS. Also (with substantial differences) in AMPH.

43   *Have no fear...* NOVEL, Isaiah 43:1f. Also in AMPH.

43   *It is said: "When Israel saw...* The Biblical passage (Exodus 14:31) referring to the crossing of the Sea of Reeds (or Red Sea), is NOVEL (also in AMPH). The passage following, about the ministering angels, is from the Babylonian Talmud, Megillah 10b. It is MODERN, first used in the 1962 edition of the ULPS Haggadah, p.10, and used subsequently in many Haggadot.

44   *O God, teach us...* NEW, by CS. Also in AMPH.

44   *That day is not yet...* NEW, by JDR. Also (with a slight difference) in AMPH.

44   *Fear not...* NOVEL, Isaiah 41:10. Also in AMPH.

44   *Whoever battles with monsters...* NOVEL, by Friedrich Nietzsche.

45   *Blessed is the One...* TRAD., first found in SRA, p. 114. The traditional text goes on to quote Genesis 15:13f.

45   *In each generation ...* TRAD, first found in the Mishnah, Pesachim 10:5. The quotation is Exodus 13:8.

45   *For the Holy One...* TRAD., a continuation of the preceding, but first found in SRA, p.114. The quotation is Deuteronomy 6:23.

45   *If you put a chain...* NOVEL, by Ralph Waldo Emerson, in the essay "Compensation."

46   *How many gifts...* TRAD. & MODERN. The traditional text, which concludes with the building of the Temple, is first found in SRA, p. 115. In our version it is abridged but supplemented with five new verses, relating to the Prophets and post-biblical times. Similar attempts to bring this composition "up to date" are to be found in the 1962 version of the ULPS Haggadah and in NUH. Also in AMPH.

48   *If we were delivered...* NEW, by CS.

48   *What constitutes the bulwark...* NOVEL, by Abraham Lincoln.

49   *Therefore we thank...* TRAD., first found in the Mishnah, Pesachim 10:5.

50   *It is by the goodness...* NOVEL, from a passage by Mark Twain, in *Pudd'nhead Wilson's New Calendar*, XX.

50   *Whatever the human law...* NOVEL, by Henry David Thoreau.

50   *The dove came back...* NOVEL, from the Midrash, Songs of Songs, Rabbah 4:2.

51   *Halleluyah...* TRAD. The custom of reciting the Hallel ("Praise") Psalms (113-18) during the Seder is mentioned already in the Mishnah, Pesachim 10:6f.

52   *When Israel went forth...* TRAD., Psalm 114. See preceding Note.

53   *I will deliver you...* NEW, by CS.

53   *We raise our cups...* MODERN. See the Note to the drinking of the First Cup, p. 7.

53   *We praise You... Redeemer of Israel.* TRAD., known as G'ulah, "Redemption," first cited in the Mishnah, Pesachim 10:6. Our version is slightly abridged, omitting a phrase about the hoped-for restoration of the sacrificial cult.

53   *We praise... vine.* TRAD. See corresponding Note to the wine benediction on p. 8.

54   *This Matzah is called...* NEW, by CS and JDR, quoting Psalm 31:10. Also in AMPH. The Mishnah (Pesachim 10:8) makes a mysterious statement which, in our Haggadah, is translated: "We conclude the Pesach meal with Afikoman." It is the answer given to the Wise Child. It could just as well have been translated: "We do *not* conclude the Pesach meal with Afikoman." The Babylonian Talmud (Pesachim 119b) records a debate between the third century teachers Rav and Samuel on the meaning of this passage of the Mishnah. Rav takes it to mean that we are not to go "from company to company," i.e., from one Seder to another; Samuel holds it to be a prohibition against a "savory" or "dessert" at the end of the Seder (for that would tend to take away the lingering flavor of the symbolic dishes, especially the Matzah). In 1925, Robert Eisler suggested that "Afikoman" comes from the Greek *aphikomenos*, meaning "the one who comes," i.e., the Messiah. This suggestion was subsequently revived by Professor David Daube in 1966, in a lecture later published in a pamphlet.

56   *A Pilgrim Song...* TRAD. The custom of chanting Psalm 126 before the Thanksgiving for the Meal on Sabbaths and Festivals has been traced back to the year 1603 (Abrahams, p. 208).

56 *Let us praise God…* TRAD. This and the following introductory formulae are cited already in the Mishnah (Berachot 7:3) and Talmuds (Jerusalem Berachot 7:2; Babylonian Berachot 45a-b, 49b-50a).

57 *Sovereign God… who live.* TRAD., the first of the four benedictions constituting *Birkat Hamazon*, the "Thanksgiving for Food." Derived from Deuteronomy 8:10, this institution is mentioned already in Josephus (*Wars of the Jews*, II, 8:5). The text is first cited in the Babylonian Talmud (Berachot 48b).

57 *For this good earth… and for its sustenance.* Amen. TRAD., the second of the four benedictions. The quotation is Deuteronomy 8:10. For the traditional "the covenant You have sealed into our flesh" we have substituted "…into our hearts" (cf. Deuteronomy 10:16 and 30:6), so that the phrase may be appropriately recited by men and women alike. Also in AMPH.

58 *Eternal God, Source of our being… rebuild Jerusalem.* Amen. TRAD., the third of the four benedictions, slightly abridged. In the interpolation for the Sabbath we have substituted "the consolation of Your people and the building of Your City" for "the consolation of Your city Zion and the rebuilding of Your holy city Jerusalem," in order to make explicit the broader, symbolic meaning implicit (not to the *exclusion* of the narrower, literal meaning) in these references to Zion and Jerusalem, and to suggest that the last two sentences of the benediction should be so understood.

59 *We praise… bless Your people with peace.* TRAD. This benediction, the last of the four, lacks a concluding eulogy. We provide an abridged version. According to the Talmuds (Jerusalem Ta'anit 4:5; Babylonian Berachot 48b, Ta'anit 31a) it was introduced after the Bar Kochba rebellion of 132-135 C.E.; but many sentences, especially those beginning "Merciful One" were inserted much later, in the Middle Ages and subsequently (see Abrahams, pp. 209 f.). The text includes allusions to Proverbs 3:4 and Job 25:2, and ends with Psalm 29:11.

62 *We raise our cups…* MODERN. See the Note to the drinking of the first cup, p. 7.

62 We praise . . . vine. TRAD. See corresponding Note to the wine benediction on p. 8.

63 *Praise…* TRAD. Here the recitation of Hallel (see Note to p. 51) is resumed, traditionally, with Psalms 115-118. We, however, omit Psalms 115 and 116, for it is customary to omit these Psalms on the last six days of Pesach, one reason being that, on account of the drowning of the Egyptians in the Red Sea, we should restrain our rejoicing on the principle of "Do not rejoice when your enemy falls" (Proverbs 24:17; Midrash, Pesikta d'R. Kahana, ed. Mandelbaum, II, 458). It seems to us appropriate to apply that principle in the Seder also. Following this reasoning, AMPH also omits these Psalms.

66 *All Your works shall praise You…* TRAD. This doxology, which "rounds off" the Hallel, is mentioned in the Babylonian Talmud (Pesachim 118a), where Rav Judah (third century teacher) identifies it with the "Benediction of Song" which according to the Mishnah (Pesachim 10:7) should be recited over the fourth cup of wine.

66 *The soul of every living being…* TRAD. According to the Babylonian Talmud (Pesachim 118a), R. Yochanan (third century Palestinian teacher) identified it with the "Benediction of Song" (*contra* Rav Judah—see preceding Note).

66 *When the freedom…* NOVEL, by Edith Hamilton, in *The Greek Way to Western Civilization.*

67 *A people may prefer…* NOVEL, by John Stuart Mill, in *Representative Government,* I.

68 *The Cup of Elijah…* The traditional Haggadah mandates, at this point, the drinking of the fourth cup of wine. We prefer to interpolate "the Cup of Elijah," although it is the "fifth cup" (see the next Note).

68 *The cups are refilled…* TRAD. The Babylonian Talmud (Pesachim 118a) records the view of R. Tarfon (first-second century Palestinian teacher) that there should be a *fifth* cup at the Seder; its derivation from the fifth verb of the Exodus 6:6-8 passage (one of the sources of the *four-cup* custom—see Notes to p. 6)

is first found in twelfth century sources (see Kasher, p. 94f.). Some Medieval Jewish authorities (e.g., Maimonides) considered the custom commendable but optional; others, like Abraham ben David of Posquieres, considered it obligatory (*ibid.*). The designation of the fifth cup as the Cup of Elijah is first found in a commentary (Chok Yaakov) by Jacob Reischer (1670-1733, Bohemia) on the Shulchan Aruch (O.Ch. 480, Note 6).

68   *The door is opened...* TRAD. This custom originated in the Middle Ages and was widely practiced by the sixteenth century (see Kasher, p. 180). It was both a precaution against informers (to show there was nothing to hide, in view of the "blood accusation") and an expression of trust in God's protection and of hope for the speedy coming of the Messianic age, heralded by the return of the prophet Elijah. Traditionally, a passage beginning "Pour out Your wrath..." (Psalms 79:6f., 69:25 and Lamentations 3:66) is recited; of this, we retain only Psalm 79:7, as part of the new ritual in this Haggadah.

68   *Why do we drink...* NOVEL. See first Note to p. 7.

68   *I am the Eternal One...* Exodus 6:6f. See second Note to p. 7.

69   *But there is a fifth promise...* NEW, by CS, quoting Exodus 6:8. See the corresponding passage in AMPH.

69   *The world is far...* NEW, by CS.

69   *In every generation...* TRAD., part of a longer passage that appears earlier in the Haggadah. See Note to "Blessed is the One" on p. 45.

69   *But the Holy One...* TRAD., a continuation of the preceding passage.

69   *We remember expulsions... to ash.* NEW, by CS.

70   *They have devoured...* TRAD., Psalm 79:7. See Note to "The door is opened" on p. 68.

70   *But we have saved...* NEW, by CS. A variation on the passage cited in the last Note but two.

70   *For from these fugitives...* NEW, by CS.

70   *We shall remember...* NEW, by CS. The last sentence is TRAD., from the passage beginning "We were slaves" on p. 21.

70   *We remember many glories...* NEW, by CS.

70   *Zion heard...* NOVEL, Psalm 97:8.

70   *But the full glory...* NEW, by CS and JDR.

71   *I will lift up the cup...* NOVEL, Psalm 116:13.

71   *Again, and yet again... our redemption shall begin. As it is written.* NEW, by CS, with allusions to I Kings 21 and 19.

72   *Behold, I am sending...* MODERN, Malachi 3:23f. Also in AMPH, NUH, p. 70.

72   *And on that day... Land of Promise.* NEW, by CS, quoting Exodus 6:8.

73   *Eiliyahu hanavi...* MODERN. A traditional folk song that has become associated with Pesach, on account of its connection with the figure of Elijah and the theme of redemption.

73   *Rabbi Yehoshua...* NOVEL, from the Babylonian Talmud, Sanhedrin 98a, quoting Psalm 95:7. R. Joshua ben Levi was a third century Palestinian teacher; R. Shimon bar Yochai was a second century Palestinian teacher who was at one time condemned to death by the Romans and for some years took refuge in a cave.

74   *Our celebration...* NEW, by CS. This introduces a series of Biblical verses on the theme of remembrance of our servitude in Egypt, and of the ethical lesson to be drawn therefrom. A somewhat similar reading

appears in *The New Haggadah* (Reconstructionist), Berhman House, Inc., N.Y., 1942, 1978. There it follows the Ten Plagues.

74   *As you rejoice… land of Egypt.* NOVEL, Deuteronomy 16:11f.

74   *May our remembering…* NEW, by CS. An introduction to the next passage.

74   *The strangers in your midst…* MODERN, Leviticus 19:34. Also in *The New Haggadah*, p. 54.

74   *There shall be…* NEW, by CS. An introduction to the next passage.

74   *Only Me shall the people…* MODERN, Leviticus 25:55. Also in *The New Haggadah*, p. 56.

75   *Our redemption…* NEW, by CS. An introduction to the drinking of the fourth cup. On the quotation ("I will TAKE YOU…") see the Note to the drinking of the First Cup, p. 7.

75   *We praise… vine.* TRAD. See corresponding Note to the wine benediction on p. 8.

75   *We praise… to be free.* MODERN. This is one of a series of benedictions found in the morning service, first found in the Babylonian Talmud, Berachot 60b. There, however, the present benediction is in the negative, "who has not made me a slave." The American Reform and Conservative liturgies both utilize the positive formulation, as does the (Conservative) Rabbinic Assembly's new "preliminary edition" of the Haggadah.

76   *Our Seder now concludes…* TRAD. and NEW. The Hebrew is the first stanza of a *piyyut* (liturgical poem) by Joseph ben Samuel Bonfils (eleventh century, France). The last four (English) lines are NEW, by CS.

76   *Then all shall sit…* NOVEL, Micah 4:4. Also in AMPH.

76   *For us and all Israel…* NEW and TRAD. The first two lines and the fourth are NEW, by CS, intended to make explicit the broader, universal hope, over and above the narrower, national one, that has always been implicit in the exclamation of the third line, "Next year in Jerusalem!" That line is traditionally recited immediately after the *piyyut* (see last Note but one), probably prompted by the conclusion of its second stanza (here omitted): "Soon may You lead the offshoots of Your planting, redeemed, to Zion in joy."

79   *To You praise belongs…* TRAD. A *piyyut* (liturgical poem) of unknown authorship that has been traced back to German, Italian, and English Haggadot of the thirteenth century (see Kasher, p. 189, Goldschmidt, p. 97), with an alphabetic acrostic, which the new translation (by JDR, here slightly adapted by CS) attempts to reproduce in English. Also in AMPH.

81   *Awesome One…* TRAD. A *piyyut* (liturgical poem) of unknown authorship which first appeared in Haggadot of the fourteenth century (see Kasher, p. 190, Goldschmidt, p. 97) with an alphabetic acrostic which the new translation (by JDR, here substantially revised by CS) attempts to reproduce in English. We have changed the phrase *yivneh veito b'karov*, "soon may He rebuild His Temple," to *yigaleinu b'karov*, rendered here as "soon may You redeem us," and the refrain *b'nei beit'cha b'karov*, "rebuild Your Temple speedily," to *p'dei am'cha b'karov*, "save Your people speedily." Also in AMPH.

82   *God of might…* MODERN. A poem by Rabbi Gustav Gottheil (1827-1903, Germany, England, and the United States), used in many Reform and Liberal Haggadot. This version goes back to the 1955 edition of SPJH. The first line of the third stanza is new, by CS.

84   *Who knows one…* TRAD. A composition of unknown authorship that has been traced back to the fifteenth century and was probably modeled on earlier, non-Jewish prototypes (see Kasher, p. 190, Goldschmidt, p. 98).

88   *Bring near the day* ("Kareiv Yom")... TRAD. The last stanza of a *piyyut* (liturgical poem) by Yannai, who probably lived in Palestine in the sixth or seventh century. Its inclusion in the Haggadah dates from about the twelfth century (see Kasher, p. 188, Goldschmidt, p. 96).

88   *Where has your love gone* ("Ana Halach Dodeich")... NOVEL, Song of Songs 6:1f. Included here, like the next two songs, because the Songs of Songs is traditionally read during Pesach (see Note to p. 10). Also in AMPH.

89   *My beloved is mine* ("Dodi Li")... NOVEL, Song of Songs 6:3, 4:9, 3:6, 4:16. Also in AMPH.

89   *I went down to the grove* ("El Ginat Egoz")... NOVEL, Song of Songs 6:11, 7:12f., 4:16. Also in AMPH.

90   *Let my people go*... MODERN. This North American Negro spiritual is found in a number of modern Haggadot. Also in AMPH.

90   *Chad Gadya*... TRAD. A composition of unknown authorship in somewhat impure Aramaic that has been traced back to the fifteenth century but was probably modeled on earlier, German prototypes (see Kasher, pp. 109f., Goldschmidt, p. 98). Its theme is paralleled by a number of passages in Rabbinic Literature—Mishnah Avot 2:6; Midrash, Genesis Rabbah 38:13; Babylonian Talmud, Bava Batra 10a.